The Cruising Yachtsman's Navigator

by the same author

Broadsmanship
Business and the Language Barrier *(with Rosemarie Jones)*
Business Books 1976
Cruising Yachtsman's Troubleshooter

The Cruising Yachtsman's Navigator

Richard Simpkin

Illustrated by John Bradley

Stanley Paul, London

Stanley Paul & Co Ltd
3 Fitzroy Square, London W1P 6JD

An imprint of the Hutchinson Publishing Group

London Melbourne Sydney Auckland
Wellington Johannesburg and agencies
throughout the world

First published 1978

Set in Monotype Times New Roman

Printed in Great Britain by litho at
The Anchor Press Ltd, and bound by
Wm Brendon & Son Ltd, both of
Tiptree, Essex

ISBN 0 09 132830 6 (cased)
132831 4 (paper)

Contents

List of Illustrations

Figures

Photographs

Acknowledgements

I want to record my warmest thanks to the many people who have helped in the preparation of this book – my wife and staff; my illustrator who dealt so patiently with my infantile doodles; numerous sailing friends; the firms I approached, most notably John Bainbridge of Electronic Laboratories Ltd, Ernie Barlex and Colin Wagstaff of Henry Browne & Son Ltd and A. Gwyn Johns of Thomas Walker & Son Ltd; David Bartlett of Thomas Reed Publications Ltd; and, though public servants must remain anonymous, the Hydrographer of the Navy and his staff, many of whom went to great lengths to help me.

Introduction

My personal impression, confirmed by RYA examination statistics, is that, despite the numerous courses and publications available, navigation remains the greatest single stumbling-block for those seeking to graduate from dayboats in confined waters to wider-ranging cruising or racing. There are maybe three reasons for this: it is the one subject completely new to a dayboat sailor; it looks mathematical; and, along with ropework, it still tends to be taught and tested formally.

My aim in this book is likewise threefold: to bring together the wide range of fringe skills and knowledge that most yachtsmen need to find their way about; to pare to the bone the treatment of navigational techniques as such; and to relate all this to what is feasible in a small yacht in moderate or heavy weather. I hope what I cover will meet most of the needs of most yachtsmen. For the rest, I still know of no better books than Mary Blewitt's *Navigation for Yachtsmen* and *Celestial Navigation for Yachtsmen* (Stanford Maritime).

Let's first get the subject in perspective. The bulk of what the ordinary yachtsman does to find his way from A to B – particularly in the more dangerous stages of his passage – is pilotage or water-borne map-reading. This is very like land map-reading combined with using a gazetteer to get additional information; it is about as difficult as finding your way in a car round minor roads and identifying things of interest on the way. It is easier than using a map cross-country and not in the same league as orienteering. The navigational techniques the average yachtsman needs are about as complex as working out the time to put the Christmas turkey in the oven, cutting out a dress from a pattern or following fairly basic knitting instructions.

In this book I have reduced worked examples to a minimum, using waters I know, and left you to make up your own practice examples. This is because I believe you will do best to work on charts and a tidal atlas of waters you know, and to back up or if possible replace study with practice underway. To achieve common ground all I would ask is that you use Admiralty Charts, *Reed's Nautical Almanac*, and the Admiralty Chart 5011 (booklet form) *Symbols and Abbreviations used on Admiralty Charts* (1976 edition or later).

The likely pitfalls concern concentration and diligence rather than lack of skill. I shall be stressing these throughout the book, but I should like to fix some of them in the reader's mind straightway:

You sail at roughly the same speed as you *walk*. *Don't* be over-ambitious or over-optimistic.

You can only be as good as your information; frequently you are worse. Optimize and maximize your information.

The water your boat is in is usually moving past the land and takes you with it.

Gross mistakes on a small boat cost much time and effort and may be dangerous. Double check everything all the time.

Minor errors, on the other hand, are something you have to learn to live with.

Make sure you always know where you are. If you hit a weather, visibility or mechanical problem, you need to know this immediately.

There is nothing so valuable as local knowledge. Seek advice – but double check this too if you can.

There are occasions, notably fog, when you will need to navigate continuously and very accurately. But I believe most amateur navigators will cope best with these by using informed common sense and basic techniques with which they are familiar and which they have adapted to themselves and their working conditions.

Sooner or later you are going to be faced with a situation in which your plots either tell you with equal conviction that you are in two different places at once or assure you that you are somewhere you know you are not. To get out of messes like these you need a gradually acquired understanding, based on experience, of what actually goes on when you navigate a small boat – an informed seat to your pants rather than a pocket calculator or a book of rules.

I hope this book will add to the scope, safety and pleasure of your sailing.

1
Information

Roads have sign-posts and ground reveals itself to the eye; the sea has none and does not. Today a vast amount of information on most waters is available to the navigator who takes the trouble to acquire and use it. As you sit back smugly having just accomplished a difficult entry with the aid of charts, sailing directions and marks – and of your instruments – just try to picture for a moment the mariners of old with crude charts, few instruments and no marks; and particularly the first person to find the channel. You will then realize just how heavily you depend on information. And it must be good information. The only serious mishap I have had so far was due to out-of-date information; one of two channels through a bar had closed right up since my chart and sailing directions were printed. Although they were very recent, I had failed to confirm that no change had occurred.

Theory and human experience agree in affirming that too much information is better than too little; in fact unless you have redundant information you are unlikely to see the full picture – let alone to be able to double check it. Navigating experience will give you the judgement to grade information for accuracy and reliability, which are not quite the same thing. This chapter discusses how you can assemble and update the information you need, and the value of local sources.

Charts

Types of chart

For British waters you have a choice between Admiralty charts and commercial 'yachtsmen's' charts. Admiralty charts cover many other areas too, and in most waters you have a choice between the official charts of the nation concerned and the commercially produced ones. Even if you speak the language of the legend of a foreign chart, the abbreviations and symbols may cause problems. However the *Yachtsman's Eight-Language Dictionary* by Barbara Webb (Adlard Coles) is of great help here, and the European standardization of marks (Chapter 4) will also make life easier.

The commercial 'yachtsmen's' charts are cheaper (at the time of writing), smaller, designed to fold like a map and thus easier to handle. Despite all this, and without wishing to decry yachtsmen's charts, I would most strongly advise readers to learn their navigation from and to use Admiralty charts (or the equivalent in other countries). They provide much more information, and do so in a rigorously standardized way. Admiralty Chart 5011 (booklet form), *Symbols and Abbreviations used in Admiralty Charts*, gives you a complete clue to every marking on any Admiralty chart; we shall be probing this aspect further in Chapter 3. The very full information Admiralty charts give is often important because it tells you what shipping is likely to do, and it always makes the passage more interesting. For the same reasons that they are difficult to handle in the cockpit, Admiralty charts are the easier kind to use on an improvised or purpose-designed chart-table.

Probably the best balance is to use Admiralty charts for your full and emergency chart cover (see below), and to supplement these with yachtsmen's charts for pilotage and particularly for waters where no official chart cover, or at least no large-scale official chart cover, exists. Admiralty charts and publications are listed in Hydrographer of the Navy catalogues (home edition NP 91, world-wide NP 131).

Scales of chart

Official charts are of standard width with occasional variations of height. Their scale is therefore adjusted to cover within these dimensions an area of water that represents a useful chunk of navigational information (e.g. the group of shipping routes between East Anglia/the Thames and Belgium/Holland). We can however distinguish three categories of chart. Scales are given, as they now mostly are on maps, as *Representative Fractions* (RFs), such as 1:100000. This means that 1 cm on the chart represents 100000 cm or 1 km on the ground. To home you in on this, the RF of the old inch-to-the-mile Ordnance Survey maps was 1:63360 and the new metric equivalent is 1:50000.

Category	*Range of scale (RFs)*	*Typical purposes*
Large-scale	up to 1:50000	Harbours and approaches
Medium-scale	1:50000 to 1:500000	Sectors of coastline, short shipping routes (e.g. Harwich–Hook)
Small-scale	generally over 1:500000	Seas or parts of them, parts of oceans (e.g. English Channel, Eastern Section)

For a typical cruise, as we shall see, you will need one small-scale chart, a medium-scale chart for each coastwise leg or landfall and a large-scale chart for each port or group of ports. Harbour plans are sometimes grouped and sometimes shown as insets on medium-scale charts.

Full and emergency chart cover

It is never easy to decide the chart cover you need. There is a real dilemma between being caught out (there are few worse feelings, especially in bad weather!) and holding a library of charts that you cannot afford to keep up to date. By the time this book is out, Admiralty charts will largely have gone metric and most of the European waters used by yachts will have changed to the new buoyage system. One can therefore hope the charts will remain up to date, or at least within the scope of hand amendment, for some time except in the known areas of shifting channels and bottoms. Since an out-of-date chart is usually better than no chart at all, I am inclined to stick my neck out and recommend what most yachtsmen in fact do: update or renew working charts as they need them and do their best to amend the rest, accepting that some of their emergency cover is a bit out of date. On the other hand, a small expenditure on charts is a very cheap form of insurance premium; cover of your emergency area can be restricted to small-scale plus large-scale for key refuge ports.

You need *full chart cover* of the area you *intend* to sail in, and *emergency cover* of everywhere to which you may be *forced to go* from any point in the full-cover area. Let us look at two examples.

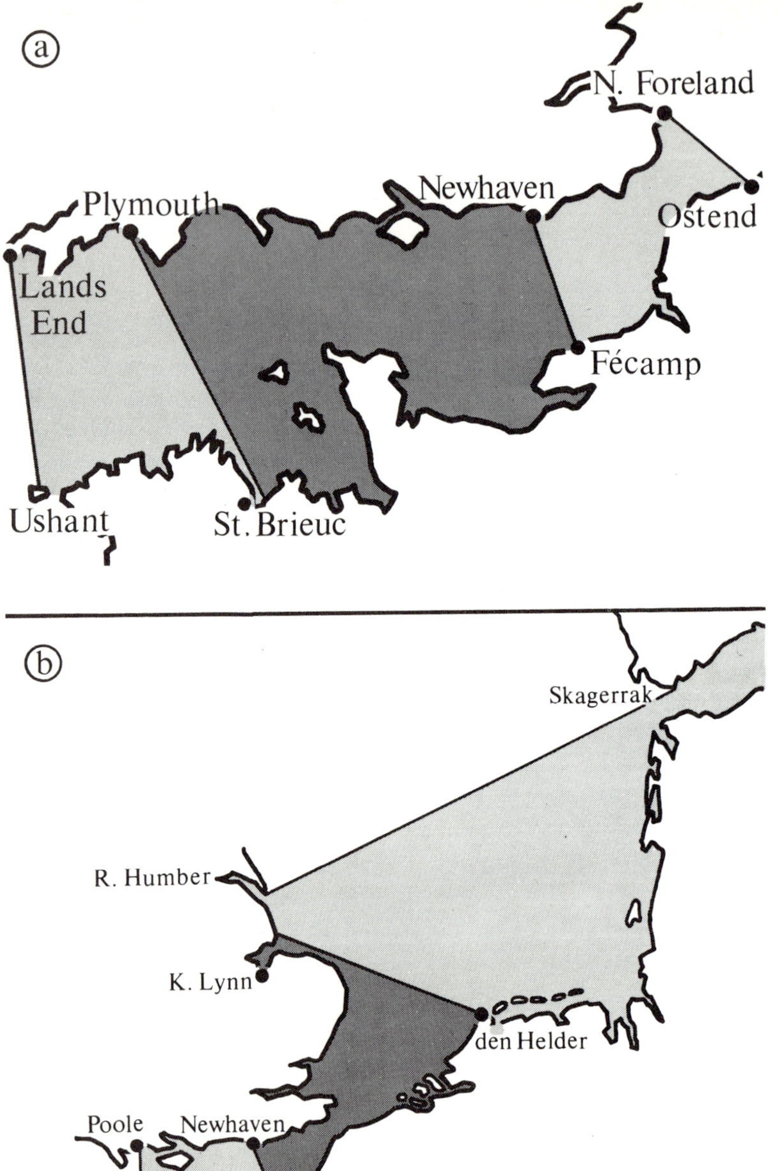

Figure 1. *Chart cover.*
(a) Poole-based.
(b) Norfolk-based.

A yacht is based at Poole and, as in fact most yachts are, used mainly for local cruising with excursions in various directions across the Channel and along both its coasts. I would opt for full chart cover for the area enclosed by Plymouth, Newhaven, Fécamp, St Brieuc (Figure 1*a*). Since the Channel contains several areas of semi-sheltered waters (e.g. the Solent) and a number of easy, all-weather ports, I would regard it as sufficient to extend emergency cover only to North Foreland–Ostend in the East and Land's End–Ushant in the West. This gives a ratio of full to emergency cover of rather under 2:1 by area.

Now consider the same yacht based on the Norfolk coast, with full cover for the area Newhaven–King's Lynn–den Helder, etc.–Dieppe (Figure 1*b*). In an Easterly blow, there is no safe port between Harwich and the Humber. And it is interesting to speculate where a Westerly, particularly the not improbable sustained South-westerly, might take one. One really needs some cover to the East right out to the Skagerrak and Hamburg, while to the West Poole–Cherbourg should suffice. In this case the ratio of full to emergency cover approaches 4:1.

I hope the above makes clear that the chart cover you need depends on your own and your boat's capabilities, your intentions, your base, and the characteristics of sea and weather in the waters you aim to sail.

Care of charts

Once the current major changes are over, your charts should last you quite a while with hand amendment. Care of them therefore becomes important, and doubly so in a club or charter boat, where the basic charts may get literally worn out in a season. Yachtsmen's charts should have their folds reinforced with Sellotape on the back and be kept correctly folded in a bookshelf. Admiralty and other official charts are designed to lie flat in a specially designed folio in a chart-drawer or on a chart-shelf. When the charts are correctly folded and inserted their names will be visible at the front edge of the folio. To save time and minimize handling, charts should be serially numbered and stowed in the order of serial numbers, and an up-to-date list of charts by serial number kept handy on a millboard.

For using Admiralty charts above decks you should provide yourself with a large, tough transparent plastic envelope; the transparent type of plastic map-case with zip closure is ideal. And you should always keep the chart tucked under a cushion or otherwise secured so that it does not blow away.

After each passage the charts used should be cleaned (preferably with an art gum eraser – see also page 44), any unofficial creases or folds smoothed out and the charts restored to their proper stowage positions.

Sailing directions

For the cruising man, sailing directions are any form of leaflet or book which provides relatively permanent navigational information – by contrast with almanacs, etc., the purpose of which is to provide data that changes from year to year. A particularly important document in most waters is the *tidal atlas*; this gives information on the direction and strength of tidal streams and will be explored fully in Chapter 6.

As with charts, you have a choice between official publications, such as Admiralty pilots and lists of lights, and informative books. In fact the yachtsman needs both. In the Channel for instance you need both the *Channel Pilot* (Hydrographer of the Navy, NP 27) and Adlard Coles' *Channel Harbours and Anchorages*. The Admiralty pilots are reissued every ten to fifteen years, with supplements every two to three years in between. Unofficial publications are revised as the economics of publishing allow; for the better sellers, every three to four years. Then you have local sailing directions published by clubs (e.g. *Sailing Directions and Anchorages, Orkneys*, Clyde Cruising Club) as well as the comprehensive handbooks published, for instance, by the (British) Cruising Association and the Irish Cruising Club (see Bibliography, page 198).

You need to have a clear idea of the respective roles of these various kinds of book. The official publications are authoritative and, if updated and used in conjunction with Admiralty charts, are comprehensive, reliable and accurate. They give good descriptions of navigational lights and they are sometimes the sole source of the 'traffic light' or other code used to control entry to and exit from a harbour. On the other hand much of the information in them is irrelevant for the yachtsman. The unofficial books are more directly helpful in every respect – approach, entrance, anchorage/moorings and facilities – but there is no obligation on the author or publisher to ensure that they are accurate or up-to-date. In my view the yachtsman who gets into difficulties by working entirely off unofficial books, invaluable as they are, has only himself to blame. Before entering a strange port, you should read it up in both kinds of publication – and of course study it on the medium- and large-scale charts (see Chapters 4, 8 and 16).

We shall be discussing mistakes and errors in Chapter 7, but this may be a good moment to explain the distinction I drew above between 'accuracy' and 'reliability' of information. Consider the following statement: 'You will find 2 m of water 1 cable ESE of this mark even at low water springs' (i.e. the lowest normal level of the water). If I draw 1·5 m and go aground 1 cable ESE of this mark, subsequently finding good water 50 m further from it, I would (after a suitable flow of expletives) describe the information as 'inaccurate', corresponding to what I shall call an 'error'. If I found I could not get through at low water anywhere to the east of the mark in question, I should (after a rather fuller description of the author) call it 'unreliable', corresponding to a 'mistake'. Information in the texts and diagrams of unofficial books is often inaccurate and occasionally unreliable. As I have learnt the hard way on both scores, such information must be double checked on official publications and charts. Yet without this unofficial information, one would waste much time and effort trying to behave like a big ship and would completely miss out on many fascinating things that are possible for yachts but not for commercial shipping.

The rule must therefore be: brief yourself to the hilt from unofficial documentation, but do your actual navigating from up-to-date official charts and books.

Almanacs

For almanacs, read *Reed's Nautical Almanac* – I have never met a Europe-based English-speaking yachtsman who used any other, and many Continental yachtsmen use it despite the language barrier. *Reed's* is a splendidly planned mine of first-rate information. As it is a bit overwhelming on first acquaintance, let me take you through it (using the 1977 edition – there are slight variations in layout from year to year).

Right at the beginning you find a 'Personal Index' containing a few key entries and spaces for you to enter the pages you most often use. Then follow illustrations of buoyage systems (cross-referenced to the full explanation), signal flags and the Morse code. Then you come to the List of Contents. You start with Notices to Navigators (late corrections); around here you will find a tear-out order form which you send in to get (free) the Half-Yearly Supplement, containing further corrections from 1 September (1976) to 1 March (1977) plus any additional information (e.g. the buoyage change-over programme). Then comes the almanac proper (from which you get sunrise, sunset and the two twilights), followed by 170-odd pages of basic seafaring knowledge.

At the beginning of Section X you find a list of harbour-masters' telephone numbers and then (X and XI) full details of entry requirements for UK and Continental ports. Section XII on Radio Aids to Navigation is a key one (Chapter 13 in this book). The three sections you will probably use most are: XIV, Tides and Tidal Streams, which includes a compact, simplified tidal atlas; XXI, Weather Forecasting; and XXVI and XXVII, Visual Navigation Aids for the UK, and for the Continent.

Note particularly that there are three indexes (all normally on yellow paper). The first is the Tides and Lights Index, port by port; note that this has three references – one for tides, one for lights and one for entry signals, etc. The second is the index of key reference tables, and the third is the general index. *Reed's* is corrected up to the time of going to press, the date and number of the last *Notices to Mariners* being given, and again updated to 1 March by the Half-Yearly Supplement. You should, however, always carry ample charts for the area in which you are cruising and be certain to have them corrected before commencing a voyage. This is most important at any time but particularly during the next few years when so many navigational aids are being changed. Once again, you should check all data from two independent sources whenever you can.

Updating

The expense of renewing one's complete library of charts and navigational books every year will be too much for most. As already stressed, priority must go to the documentation most frequently used. The *sine qua non* is to buy a new *Reed's Nautical Almanac* each year, as opposed to trying to work with an old *Reed's* and new local tide tables. Second come charts, but these need not always be renewed. Certainly the recent change-over to metric soundings and the new buoyage system calls for new charts as these become available; but typical year-to-year amendments can be made by hand (and are in fact so made on stocks of charts). Next I would rate as essential the purchase of supplements to Admiralty pilots and lists of lights, and of new editions of these when issued. This keeps your hard navigational data up to date.

My own policy is not to renew the unofficial background books until they become so wildly obsolete as to become unmanageable, but to annotate my copies from first-hand (and occasionally vicarious) experience, cross-referencing these to notes in the log. For waters not fully covered by official publications, I prefer to update from first-hand information or from consulting local experts. This brings us to the two sources of up-to-date information.

Notices to Mariners

You can obtain a regular monthly package of *Notices to Mariners* at the cost of the postage (£3 in 1976). This can be arranged with chandlers who are agents for Admiralty publications or through harbour-masters/Coastguards. These documents, rather like a computer printout, will present you with a vast flow of paper, 99 per cent of which will be of no interest. But the other 1 per cent may be literally vital and is quite easy to pick out. This is the source from which to keep your charts, Admiralty publications and *Reed's* fully amended. Don't try to do more amending then you really need, or you will get swamped and fall down on the essentials.

Local sources

I have already stressed the value of local knowledge and mentioned the list of harbour-masters' telephone numbers in *Reed's*. You will also find there lists of Coastguard stations. *Don't hesitate* to ring these people up, or to call them up if you and they have RT on a common non-emergency frequency. They will not think you foolish or cowardly. Theirs is a fairly lonely job anyway, and for every reason they would far sooner talk over weather or channel problems and give advice than have to set up a rescue operation. (Conversely, if you have said you are coming and change your mind through whim or weather, let them know this as soon as you can.)

Let me reinforce this last point with an example. After battling my way through Norfolk Broads traffic, lowering the mast, dealing with the problems of raising it and getting ready for sea in Yarmouth Haven, I like to catch the tide to Southwold and relax for a tide or night before starting the cruise proper. Southwold has a shallow sand bar with a shifting channel. The approach bearing varies between 290°M and 340°M, and a lumpy sea running after a Northerly can make the entrance dangerous. Therefore, well as I know this little port, I always ring the harbour-master to check bearing and conditions – and again to recheck the bearing if I am delayed twenty-four hours.

Let this example also serve to drive home the fact that the navigator's life-blood is information – hard, clear-cut, up-to-date information. Some might argue that training and experience reduce the importance of the quality and quantity of data; I would prefer to think that trained instincts and an experienced eye are an important complement to information, serving to plug some of the inevitable gaps.

2

Instruments

I have always been surprised that, with a few individual exceptions such as Colas's schooner in the 1976 Observer Transatlantic Race, no restriction has been placed on the instrumentation of racing yachts. The burgee has been replaced by a masthead instrument cluster, and the skipper or sailing master sits below and gives orders to his helmsman and deck-hands over the intercom. Needless to say, boats that are not fully instrumented have little chance of consistent success – the instruments give an edge in speed and precision of response. By contrast the advantage to the cruising man of lavish instrumentation is insignificant; and it is more than offset by three considerations.

One of these is quite simply *cost*: a full set of first-class instruments can represent 15 per cent of the total cost of a new ocean-racer. It is worth noting as a yardstick here that at a time when the SEAFIX (described below) cost under £32 the installed cost of its cheapest competitor, offering similar facilities but less versatility, was £235.

The second is *reliability*. If, for instance, an electromagnetic speedometer/log goes on the blink it deprives you not only of your basic dead-reckoning input (Chapter 14) but also of your dead-reckoning datum – not to mention the charming job of checking out the sensor heads under way in a heavy sea and probably collecting a bilgeful of water. On the one occasion I have used such an instrument (not the make illustrated) it broke down on every passage; fortunately we were using a patent log (see below) as a back-up, until I managed to carry away the line on a lobster-pot, after which an unfortunate character had to sit and watch the digital display constantly when we were out of sight of land.

The third consideration is one of *philosophy*, and more particularly of elegance. The instruments I shall describe below are mainly those I actually use on my own boat. In fairness I must point out that there are other makes and models on the market, but I prefer these because their design is classical, or simplified to the limit, or both – and because they are somehow attuned to my personal outlook on sailing. Each person must decide on the degree of instrumentation he wants and then shop around for the models that match both his pocket and his taste. But if my ideas on information in the previous chapter seem to be on the expensive side, the instrumentation I shall suggest is positively Spartan. Even the single cost difference mentioned above is enough to buy a complete set of documentation and keep it up to date for several years. But I would never consider cheese-paring on essential instruments at the cost of accuracy or reliability.

Barometer

Weather is a subject in its own right which I shall mainly keep out of this book. But assessing weather trends is so fundamental to navigation as well as to seamanship that the barometer must have a mention. In fact one could do worse than follow the old country-house practice of having two barometers – one for the crew to tap and one for the skipper and navigator (combined or otherwise) to use.

Since it is the direction and rate of change of pressure rather than actual pressure that matter, an unzeroed barometer is a perfectly acceptable aid. However it is a little disconcerting to work with readings differing by 10 or 20 mb. from those given on the radio, and it is worth taking or even making an opportunity to zero the instrument.

Clocks

If you are going to use celestial navigation, a second of time is equivalent to a nautical mile. Unless you are prepared to try and work direct off the radio time signal, a marine chronometer thus becomes a must – or at least did until the advent of quartz crystal watches. This book does not cover celestial navigation, but even at the lower levels you need a reasonably accurate eight-day clock and, maybe even more important, an alarm clock to make sure you get weather forecasts and take planned actions at the right time. A stop-watch is essential if you do not have a speedometer and useful in any event.

Radio

Radio is a large subject. Although even the simplest radio direction-finding (DF) sets have a broadcast reception facility, it is best to treat this as a second string and take a transistor broadcast receiver with suitable wavebands, i.e. in British waters AM (long wave) and FM (VHF). The larger portables with a horizontal ferrite AM antenna can be used for rough DF work if the DF set fails (see page 35).

A two-way RT (voice) facility that operates only on emergency frequencies is essentially a safety device rather than a navigational aid, but a set that can also be tuned to channels for general nautical traffic (Photo 1) can be extremely useful, for instance to check out a shifting channel if you are entering it after a long passage from abroad. My own view is that the cost of such a set is not justified for safety or navigational reasons in normal coastal or offshore cruising. But this may be prejudice, and there may certainly be professional or domestic reasons that justify it. To digress for a moment, I suppose

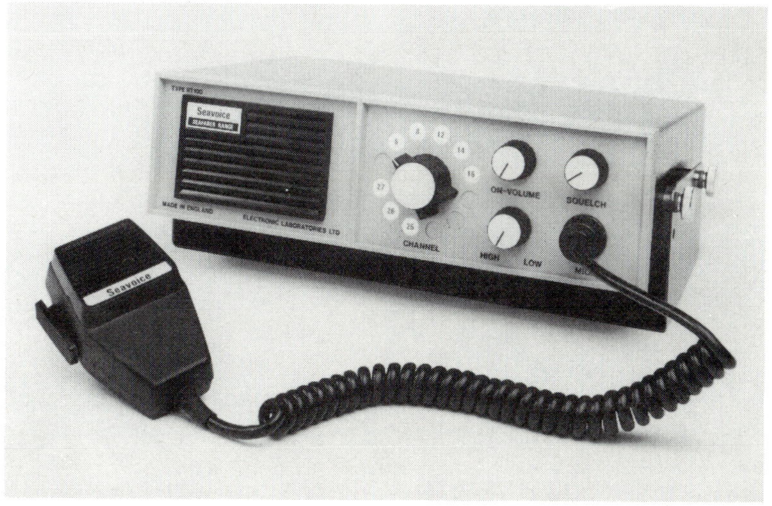

Photo 1. *A typical two-way RT set (*SEAVOICE*). (Courtesy of Electronic Laboratories Ltd, Poole.)*

one could regard two-way RT as the next step after the auxiliary engine in bringing sailing into the time-frame of modern life.

Magnetic compasses

You need three magnetic compasses on board – four if your DF radio cannot double as a hand-bearing compass (see page 35 and Chapter 12). One of these is for emergency use; it can be any good quality pocket or wrist compass, robustness and handiness being its key qualities.

Steering compass (Photo 2)

A good steering compass with effective radiant (beta) or electric illumination is a must; I prefer one with a rotatable bezel and lubber-lines. The illustration shows the compass-light socket, into which the pea-bulb and its holder are inserted; a waterproof socket on the binnacle or in the cockpit is essential. Looking at the picture you will see the compass card with its prominent North–South mark (floating in the middle) and fore-and-aft marks inscribed on the inner dome. You will also see the outer dome, mounted on a bezel with a securing device, a scale and two bold parallel lines (the lubber-lines) inscribed on the rotatable outer dome. This is called a grid.

There are two ways of using a compass of this type (Figure 2). One is to leave the lubber-lines fore and aft (scale set to 360°) and to keep the figure representing the heading ordered between these and over the forward mark on the fixed dome. The other is to set the bezel (and thus the lubber-lines) to the heading ordered and then keep the North–South line on card between and parallel with the lubber-lines. Photo 3 shows the modern 'T-grid', which prevents one from 'steering on the reciprocal' – a polite way of saying 'going

Figure 2. *Setting the lubber-lines.*

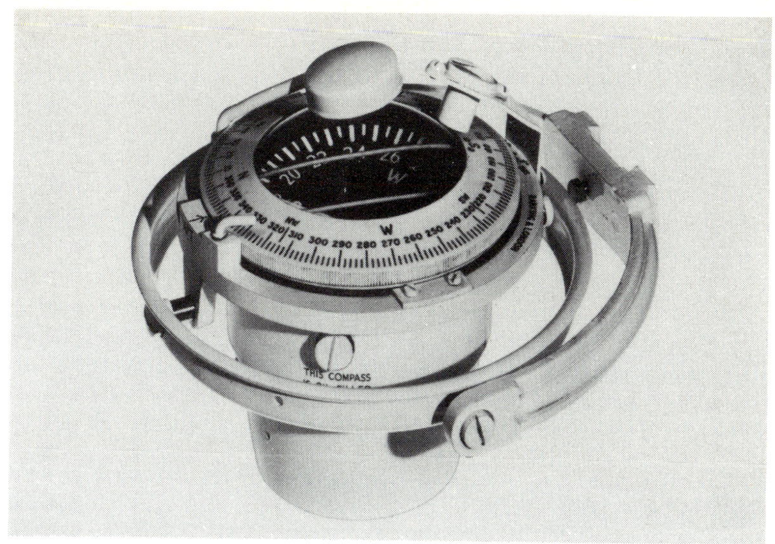

Photo 2. *Steering compass with electric illumination and lubber-lines (*SESTREL SAILING GRID*). (Courtesy of Henry Browne & Son Ltd, Barking.)*

Photo 3. *Steering compass with beta illumination (*SESTREL POPULAR GRID*). (Courtesy of Henry Browne & Son Ltd, Barking.)*

in diametrically the wrong direction'. Steering by compass will be discussed in Chapter 11.

It is important to choose a working position for the steering compass that is easy for the helmsman to use, as far as possible from any masses of iron and steel, particularly rotating masses, and reasonably protected. With wheel steering, and certainly with a centre cockpit, the compass lives in a binnacle; it is set up and corrected on installation, and a *deviation card* (Chapters 7 and 11) will probably be needed. In a tiller-steered boat with an inboard engine mounted reasonably low and forward and a wooden or GRP hull, a working position under the tiller is easy to use and may obviate the need for correctors and a deviation card; bear in mind however the possibility of heeling error. Steel or ferro-concrete hulls pose a much more serious problem with severe heeling and direct errors. Remember however that stowage in the cockpit lockers (e.g. an outboard for the dinghy, winch handles) may affect the compass. A cockpit-mounted compass must have a secured stowed position below decks; you will therefore need two mounting plates, which should be supplied with models of this kind.

Hand-bearing compass (Photo 4)

This is a high-grade prismatic compass with dry battery or beta illumination, usually mounted on a large handgrip. It is used to take bearings on other objects (Chapter 12). As can be seen, there is a V-shaped nick in the top of the prism and a line down its face; other models have a mark (or sometimes a 'bead') on the opposite side of the compass. You sight on the object by lining these up and then, if the prism is correctly adjusted, you will see either the bearing or the back-bearing (i.e. your bearing from the object) displayed in the prism. It is important to choose a model through which you personally can easily sight and read the bearing, particularly if you wear glasses. Don't try to hold the compass too close to your eye; for some individuals some compasses are best held at arm's length. If electrically illuminated, the compass should have a push-button switch so that the light does not obscure your distant vision. The hand-bearing compass is a delicate and essential instrument; being loose it is particularly liable to get damaged in a seaway. It is best to keep this compass in its case when not needed and to have a secure ready stowage position for it (a clip is provided with some models).

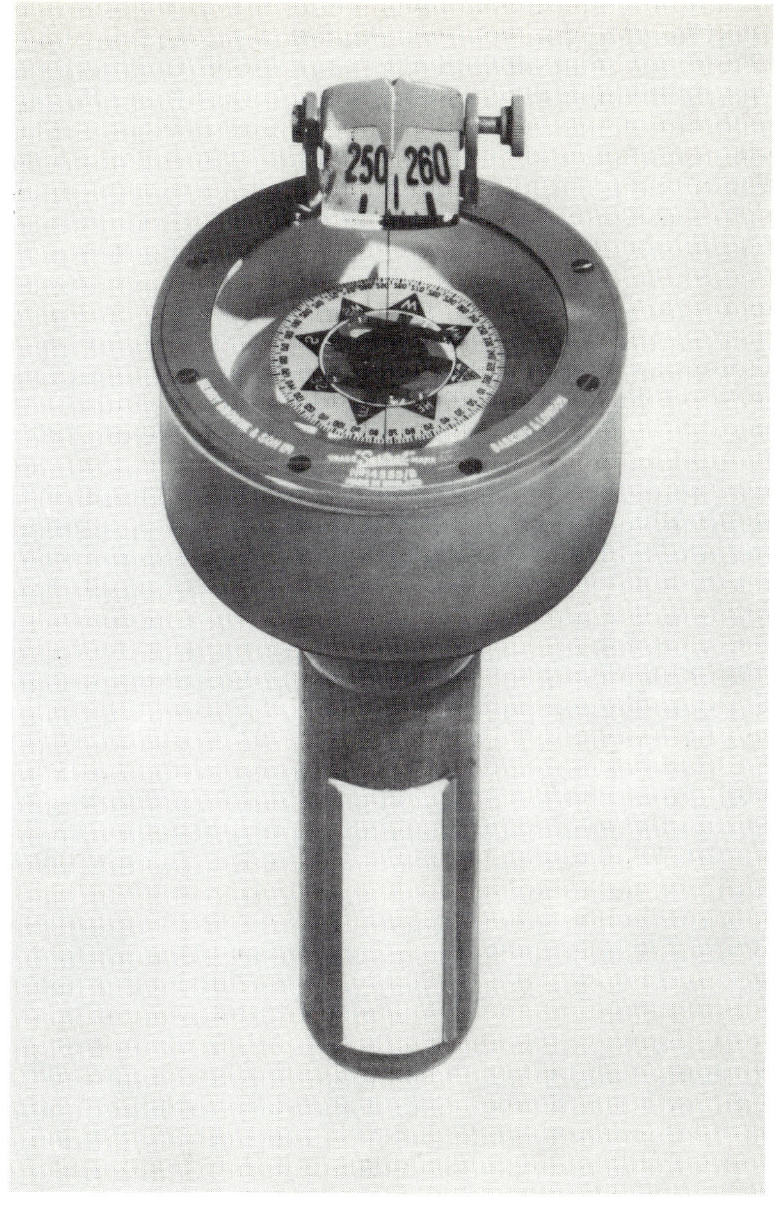

Photo 4. *A typical hand-bearing compass with beta illumination* (SESTREL RADIANT). *(Courtesy of Henry Browne & Son Ltd, Barking.)*

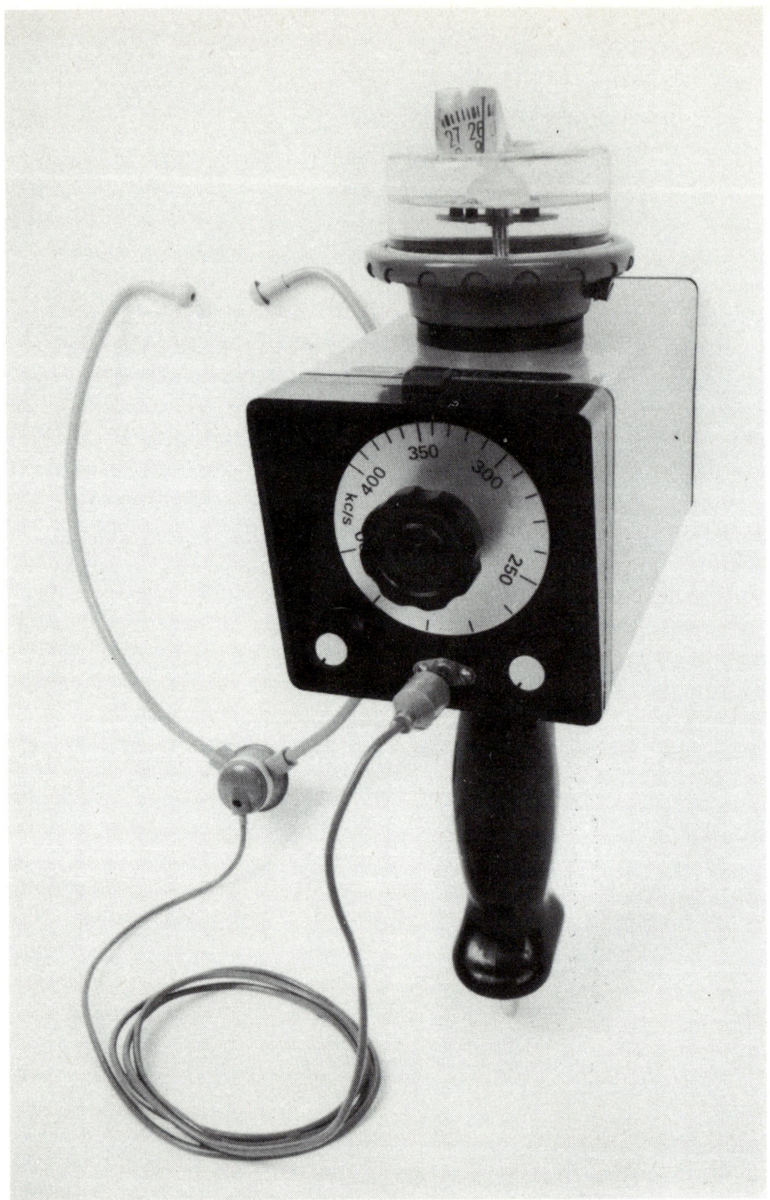

Photo 5. *The* SEAFIX *doubles as a DF radio and a hand-bearing compass. (Courtesy of Electronic Laboratories Ltd, Poole.)*

Magnetic hand-bearing compasses are virtually unusable in steel-hulled boats. In wooden- or GRP-hulled boats, the continuous steel line of pulpit rail, lifeline/stanchions, pushpit rail can give rise to quite serious errors. Positioning oneself to take bearings is further discussed in Chapter 12. The SEAFIX DF radio (below) doubles as a hand-bearing compass.

Direction-finding (DF) radios (Photo 5)

The SEAFIX is the cheapest and simplest of an enormous range of DF radios. It has a broadcast reception facility and built-in illumination, and is handy enough to serve as a hand-bearing compass. In my opinion its radio DF performance is satisfactory for coastal cruising and offshore sailing in well-beaconed waters such as the Channel or the Southern North Sea. I do not have first-hand evidence of its performance at longer ranges but without wishing to suggest any limitations I cannot believe that all those who pay ten or twenty times the price for a larger installation do so just to show off. On the other hand, long-range working with straightforward DF techniques introduces errors quite independent of the performance of the set. Personally I get better results from the small set than I do from more costly ones, but I suppose that's the perverse sort of person I am.

Use of the DF radio will be discussed in Chapter 13, but it is worth just mentioning the principle here. Switched to the 'broadcast' mode and tuned on, say, Radio 2 (1500 m), it behaves just like a normal receiver. But for DF work it is switched to the 'navigation' mode and tuned to a radio beacon. The principle is a very simple one. In the middle part of its signal, on which the bearing is taken, a beacon sends out a continuous note. (Technically this note may be of several types, but the statement remains effectively true.) We can think of this signal loosely as a series of rings emanating from the beacon as from a splash. Two of the key components of the simple DF set are a horizontal ferrite rod antenna (as in many portable broadcast receivers) and a magnetic compass superimposed on it. When the antenna (Figure 3) is at right angles to the bearing of the station, its full length is exposed to the radiation and it collects maximum power, giving a loud signal. When the antenna rod points at the station, it picks up much less radiation and the signal fades. We can adjust the volume control so that the sound becomes in-

Figure 3. *Antenna alignment and signal strength.*

audible at this angle (the 'null point'). By turning the set to the null point and reading the bearing of the compass, we obtain a magnetic bearing on the beacon.

Logs and speedometers

A log (not to be confused with the log-book) is an instrument for measuring distance travelled through the water. It may also indicate speed. If not, speed is obtained by using a stop-watch to find the time taken to cover a certain distance, say two cables (400 yards) or a nautical mile. The unit of speed is known as a knot (one nautical mile per hour), this term deriving from the original form of log.

Modern logs are of two basic kinds. The *patent log* is a mechanical device; a line fitted with a spinner and sinker is trailed behind the boat and causes the mechanism to rotate, acting rather like a speedometer cable. Photo 6 shows a well-known patent log, and Photo 7 shows the associated remote-reading speedometer. The handling and maintenance of patent logs are discussed in Chapter 14. A built-in variant of the patent log, with a firmly mounted impeller protruding on a bracket below the waterline, is occasionally used; the mounting may be retractable through the hull. The second type of log, known as the *electromagnetic*, is based on a transducer protruding through or flush with the bottom of the hull (Photo 8). This in effect measures water pressure; its signal is interpreted electronically to give a reading of speed, and this figure is integrated to record distance travelled. The patent log is far cheaper and in my experience more reliable, and I at least would not consider using the more sophisticated type on a small cruising yacht.

The one disadvantage of the patent log is that it suffers rather more severely than the electromagnetic type from *low-speed error.* At speeds through the water below 2 k (in fact probably below 2·5 k

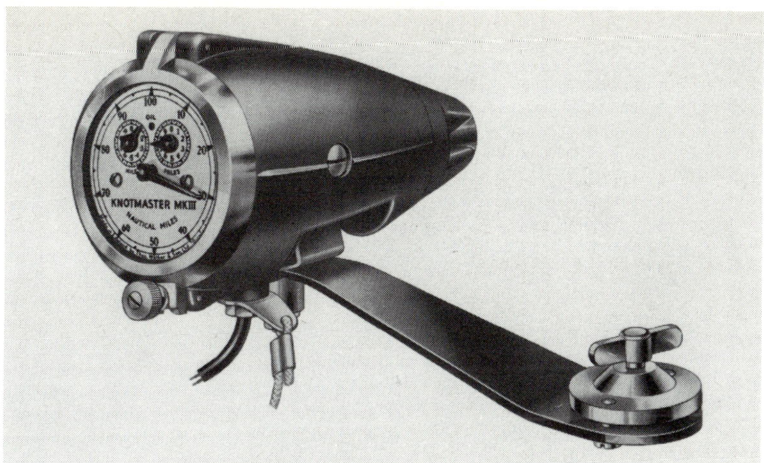

Photo 6. *A typical patent log, the* KNOTMASTER MK III. *Note securing line and electrical lead. (Courtesy of Thomas Walker & Son Ltd, Birmingham.)*

Photo 7. *The associated speedometer. (Courtesy of Thomas Walker & Son Ltd, Birmingham.)*

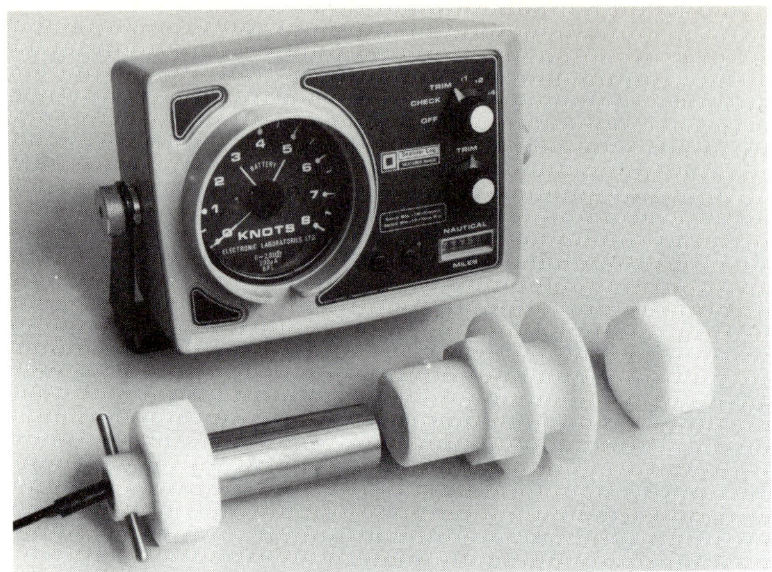

Photo 8. *An electromagnetic log (*SEAFARER*) with its retractable transducer and the associated skin-fitting. (Courtesy of Electronic Laboratories Ltd, Poole.)*

Photo 9. *A typical simple echo-sounder (*SEAFARER 3*). (Courtesy of Electronic Laboratories Ltd, Poole.)*

and in some cases 3 k or more), logs tend to read low. This can be partially overcome in the patent log by using a shorter line and a lighter sinker (or none). If your hull length and configuration are such that your maximum speed is around 6 k, you can use this shorter line permanently; otherwise you will need two lines, probably one twice the length of the other – and you should have a spare of each. Details of this method of correction are given in the manufacturer's instructions but often seem to be overlooked.

Echo-sounders and the leadline

A simple but reliable echo-sounder (Photo 9) is one instrument which I regard as indispensable. One must carry a leadline as reserve; but at best its use ties down an experienced crew member, and in the hands of someone as clumsy as myself it becomes less a means of measuring depth than an aid to creating scenes worthy of the Keystone Cops.

There are two elements in the echo-sounder – the instrument itself and a device known as a transducer fitted facing downwards through the hull and as near the bottom of the keel as possible (see Photo 8). Some boats have a transducer fitted on each side of the hull, with a manual or gravity-operated change-over switch; this minimizes inaccuracies resulting from the boat heeling. Some echo-sounders are supplied either from a dry battery or from a 12-volt (or 24-volt) system; I personally prefer the independent dry battery supply.

The echo-sounder generates a sound pulse which is by nature a pressure pulse. The transducer releases a string of pulses towards the bottom, or more precisely along its axis, and detects the echos coming back off the bottom (Figure 4). The speed of sound through water is constant, so that the time between transmission of a pulse and reception of its echo gives a measurement of depth. To the trained eye, the nature of the blip on the dial also gives useful information about the type of bottom. Very often an echo-sounder will give two or three different readings at once because of changes in depth to one side or because of the irregularities of the bottom. The correct reading is nearly always the lowest; the others can usually be tuned out by turning down the gain control.

Remember that the echo-sounder measures the depth *below the transducer*, and that a single-transducer system will read high when the boat is heeled over. Two transducers are desirable for boats with

Figure 4. *Principle of echo-sounder (sonar).*

deep fins and high angles of heel, but superfluous in most small cruising yachts. Remember also that the coaxial cable between the transducer and the instrument is a 'tuned' one; its length must not be altered.

Binoculars

Binoculars are an important aid to pilotage, their main use being to identify a feature or a buoy, if necessary by reading its name (Chapter 8). I myself like '10 × 50s'. These are binoculars which magnify ten times and which have a field of vision of around 5°. The '50' is the *light number*, which is indicative of quality and more particularly of low-light performance, and also of size. These are however about the largest glasses that you can use with the unsupported hands, and their size makes them rather liable to damage. A more compact pair, say 7 × 45 or 7 × 50, may be better for general use.

Binoculars deteriorate rapidly from damp and from surface damage to lenses. Keep them in a case, preferably with a bag of desiccant (e.g. silica gel), and use special optical tissues or at least clean, dry Kleenex-type tissues on the lenses.

Crew members who have their own binoculars should be encouraged to bring them, as this avoids the need for constant resetting of inter-ocular distance (IOD) and focus (see page 97).

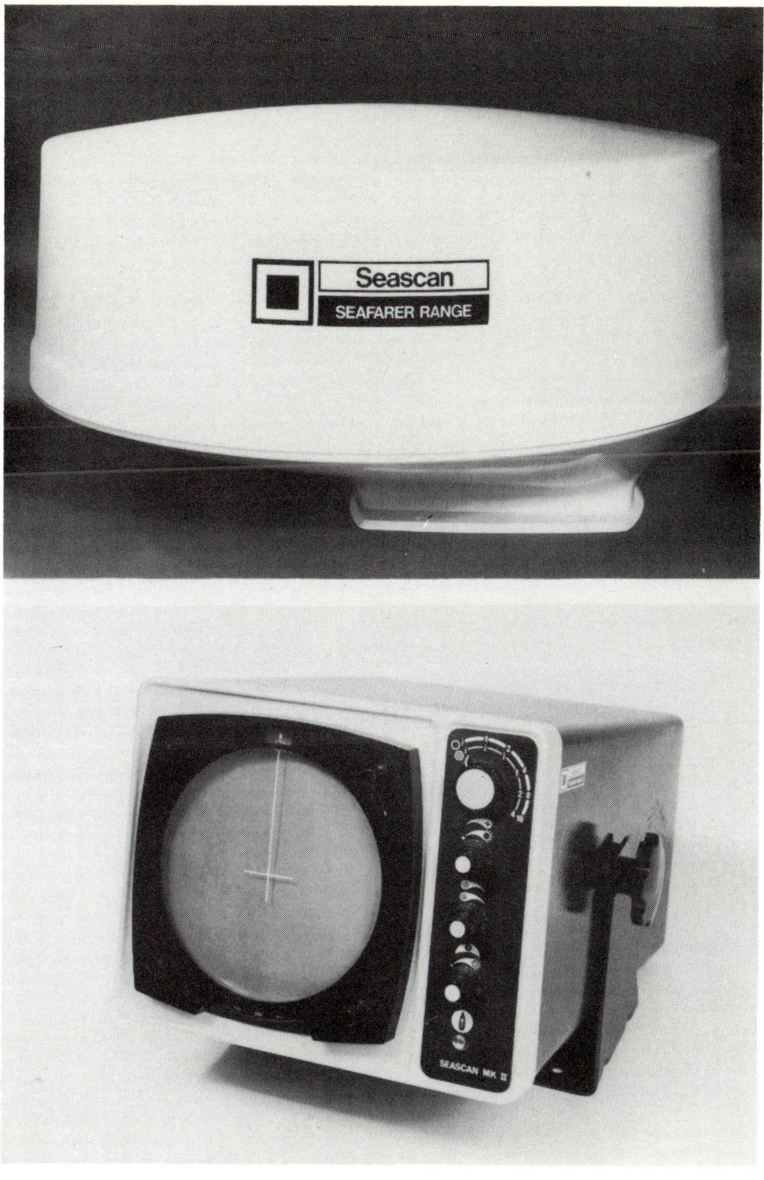

Photo 10. *A 'minimal' but satisfactory radar (*SEASCAN*);* above *antenna pack,* below *display. (Courtesy of Electronic Laboratories Ltd, Poole.)*

Radar

My own feeling is that for a small cruising yacht in bad visibility, proper use of the senses is more effective than probably unskilled use of a radar which itself may be of limited performance. The argument for radar is that without it the key sense is hearing and that in fog, so often with little or no wind, you may have to motor fairly hard to plug or at least hold against a tide. The radar shown in Photo 10 is a typical 'minimal' set. If you invest in a radar, it is worth training yourself to use it properly so that it becomes a real aid to navigation as opposed to just a safety device.

Radars may in the future become compulsory for seagoing yachts. Until they do the decision whether to invest in one must depend very much on your own feelings about it and more particularly on the nature of the waters you expect to sail in. Well-marked waters, crowded with shipping under high, well-featured coasts, make radar very valuable. By contrast its usefulness is limited in scantily marked, little-used waters lying between flat coasts or extensive mud-and-sand banks. I personally would regard a radar as considerably more valuable than two-way RT. The trouble is it *is* more valuable – it costs four to five times as much, and twenty or so times as much as the SEAFIX DF radio.

Plotting instruments

You will find various forms of circular and swinging-arm protractor on the market for the measurement of angles, and you may find one you like. A protractor is probably essential if you work with yachtsmen's charts (see page 17), but I never use any means of measuring or laying off angles except *bar-type parallel rules* (known as 'Captain Field's type') (Photo 11); I personally find the roller-type too apt to snag or slip in a seaway. One foot (presumably now 300 mm) is a comfortable length, and the ease with which the links pivot when 'walked' is a key feature.

It is handy to have a large and a small pair of *dividers*, say 200 and 125 mm, both of the single-handed type (i.e. with the two arms forming a ring at the top so that you can set them with one hand, as in Photo 12). A small (125 mm) *pair of compasses* designed to take a standard pencil is probably sufficient.

A map-reading torch is a key instrument even if you have a chart-light. This should have reasonably high magnification and cover a

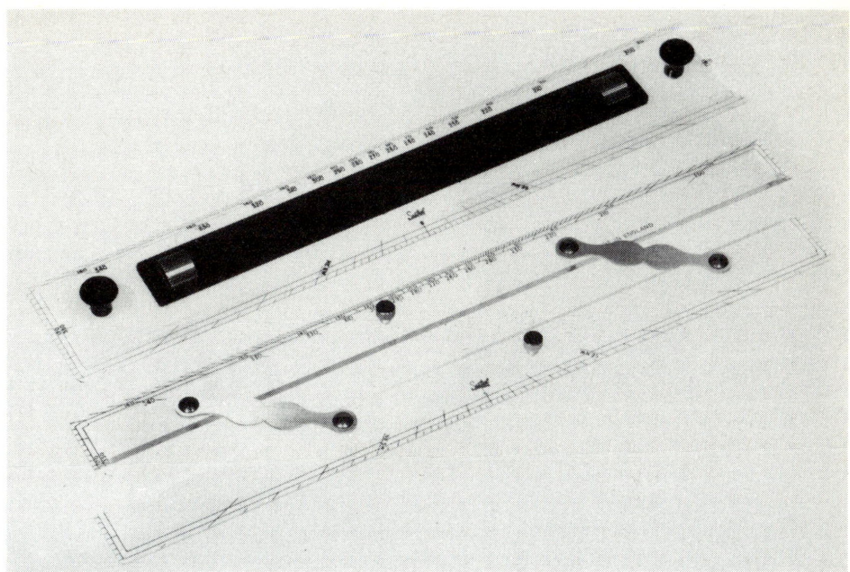

Photo 11. *Roller-type (above) and bar (Captain Field's)-type parallel rules. (Courtesy of Henry Browne & Son Ltd, Barking.)*

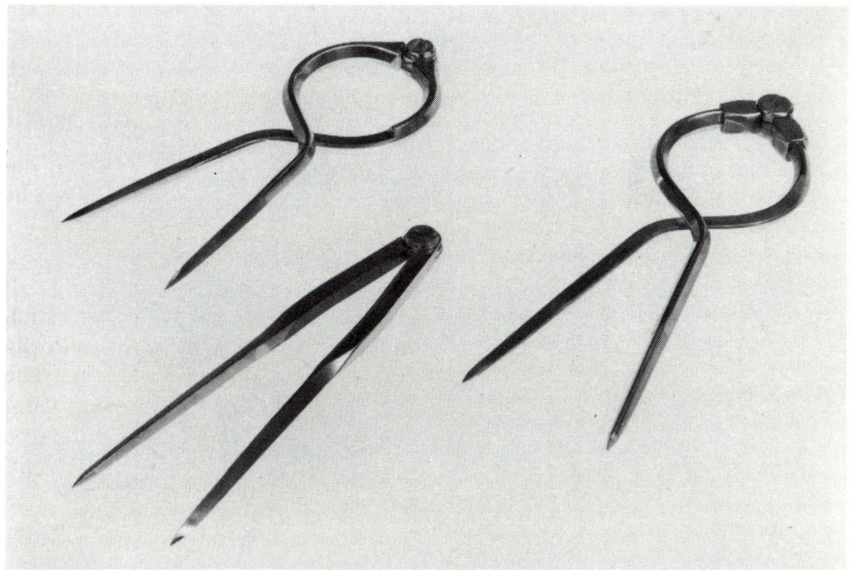

Photo 12. *Dividers: two models of the single-handed type. (Courtesy of Henry Browne & Son Ltd, Barking.)*

reasonable area – the compromise is a matter for individual choice. The types with a flat face and a normal button-and-slide switch, which can be left switched on sitting on the chart, are much more useful than the press-button models shaped to fit the hand, which are designed for rallying and night route-finding in a car.

Stationery

Having the right stationery is a surprisingly important factor in good navigation. On charts it is best to use either a hard *pencil* (say 2H) with a light touch, or a very soft one (say 3B) kept well sharpened. This is a matter of personal choice; I use a hard pencil for planning and a soft one under way. Similarly you need three kinds of *eraser*: a disc-type ink eraser (for the occasional horror), a soft india-rubber which must be kept scrupulously clean, and an art gum eraser for cleaning up charts and other documents after a passage. An ordinary ruler is often useful. These details may strike you as trivial, but unless you have just the right bits and pieces and use them carefully you will either damage the chart – maybe even blot or rub out a buoy – or make unintelligible plots.

Some regard the use of printed *weather forecast forms*, which are available in pads, as extravagant, but I find them enormously helpful especially in heavy weather or when one is tired. As a *deck-log* it is easiest to have just a lined exercise book (or large notebook); anything more formal simply slows down recording of data when the boat is bouncing about and everyone literally and figuratively has their hands full.

In my view the standard form of *log-book*, which provides for one entry every hour, is totally unsuitable for short-passage cruising. All the space covering time spent at anchor or on moorings is wasted, and I seem to have an incident every five minutes rather than the statutory one per hour when entering or clearing harbour! The detailed information you will need if any kind of dispute or claim arises should be in your deck-log (see pages 114), and most of it is of no further interest once the passage is completed without incident. The typical log-book or 'visitors' book' format is good, but one needs simply a nice-looking, well-bound book; one with plain paper on the left (for sketches and notes) and lined on the right is ideal.

3

Information Found on Charts

REFERENCES: Any medium-scale metric Admiralty chart (preferably incorporating IALA System 'A' buoyage); and *Symbols and Abbreviations used on Admiralty Charts* (Hydrographer of the Navy, Ref. 5011).

The advantages of Admiralty charts and publications were discussed in Chapter 1. I now want to look in greater depth at the information that these charts contain, apart from navigation marks, which will be covered separately in the next chapter. (I am in fact using Chart No. 2693, *Approaches to Felixstowe, Harwich and Ipswich with the Rivers Stour, Orwell and Deben*, printed 1976, with a sticker about the change to IALA buoyage. But take any metric Admiralty chart of waters you know well.) The official charts of other advanced seafaring countries tend to be similar, except of course for the language and abbreviations (see Appendix 2). Symbols are, however, standardized by the International Hydrographic Organisation and identified by a letter and a number such as G40, which signifies a lock (see Introduction to 5011).

Markings on reverse

On the back of the chart, at the centre of the lower edge, you will find the number, title and edition (i.e. month of printing). Below this in brackets you see 'Folio No. . . . Consecutive No. . . .'. Here you enter in pencil your own serial numbers. For instance the chart I have in front of me lives in my folio 1 (home waters) and in position 9 in that folio. The sequence I use within each folio is: small-scale chart(s) of area; medium-scale charts, moving away from home; and large-scale charts similarly arranged after the medium-scale chart to which they relate. At the same time as entering Folio No. 1 Consecutive No. 9 on the chart, I enter it as Serial 1/9 on my chart list. Setting up and sticking to a system saves a lot of time, temper and damage to charts. When you renew a chart, remove the old one, transferring any of your own annotations that are still valid.

Headings, notes, observations and cautions

On the front, outside the frame, you will see at diagonally opposite corners the *unit of soundings* (metres) and the *chart number*. Bottom centre is the initial date of printing and bottom left is a list of overprinted corrections. A note on cross-references to other charts and Admiralty publications is top right.

Under the title comes a further mention of the unit of soundings, followed by the *scale*, expressed as a RF (see page 19). Below that again you find the *Notes*, normally four in number:

1. The *Chart Datum* (usually 'Lowest Astronomical Tide', LAT) for Admiralty charts, which is different (e.g. Mean Low Water Springs, MLWS) on official charts of other countries. In some unused space you will find a table of Tidal Levels. The importance and interpretation of all these figures is explained in Chapter 5.
2. *Heights*. Note the distinction between drying heights and land heights. *Drying heights* are of spots or features in the intertidal zone (tinted green), and the unit figure in them is underlined. *Land heights* usually appear either along the length of contour lines (see 5011 C1) as spot-heights, or in parentheses beside the description of features, e.g. RADIO TR (83).
3. The *type of projection* and the *survey datum*, neither of which needs concern us in this book.
4. Other sources of data used.

Either below the standard notes or in any convenient space are the *Special Notes*, *Observations* and *Cautions*; these deal with specific features, restrictions and dangers. There is normally a reference to them (e.g. 'See Caution') in the area or against the feature affected.

You will also normally find a table of tidal streams at specific marked points (magenta diamonds with key letter). These are used in conjunction with a tidal atlas (Chapter 6). Other spare space may be taken up by insets of harbours, the upper reaches of rivers or dangerous areas calling for large-scale detailed cover.

Latitude and longitude grids

The chart is framed by latitude (vertical) and longitude (horizontal) scales. The whole chart is gridded at one degree (1°) to one minute of arc (1′) intervals according to scale, and the frame is broken down into interstices of 30, 10, 5 or unit seconds of arc (″).

This grid enables you to record your position or pass it by RT or other form of signal in emergencies in a way that is unambiguous and universally understood, e.g.

POSITION 51°56′36″ NORTH, 01°27′08″ EAST

Note that the nautical convention is the opposite of the land convention used by armies, surveyors, guides and orienteers, in which easting (longitude) is given first and northing (latitude) second. There are sound historical reasons for both these conventions.

The most frequent use you will make of the *latitude (vertical) grid* is to measure and lay off distances, since

1 minute of latitude = 1 nautical mile.

Some charts have *national* or *international grid references* (as used in Ordnance Survey maps, etc.) in magenta figures on the latitude and longitude scales, and the major grid-square references (two-letter groups) related to the chart in an inset.

The compass rose

Look at the compass rose on a chart or in Section U of 5011. Note that the *magnetic variation* (the difference between true and magnetic North) varies with time and place. For the yacht navigator on short and medium passages, however, if the error in the magnetic rose is large enough to affect the order of accuracy to which you are working, the chart is so old that a slightly inaccurate bearing would be the least of your problems!

As will be repeatedly stressed in this book, you can forget about true bearings. Despite their name they have no moral or other superiority for you; in fact they are a bore. One of the messages of this book is *work entirely on magnetic bearings.*

If you have to convert a bearing from true to magnetic take a pencil or ruler, lay it on the nearest convenient full rose of your chart against the true bearing (Figure 5), making sure the edge you are using passes through the centre. Mark the position where the

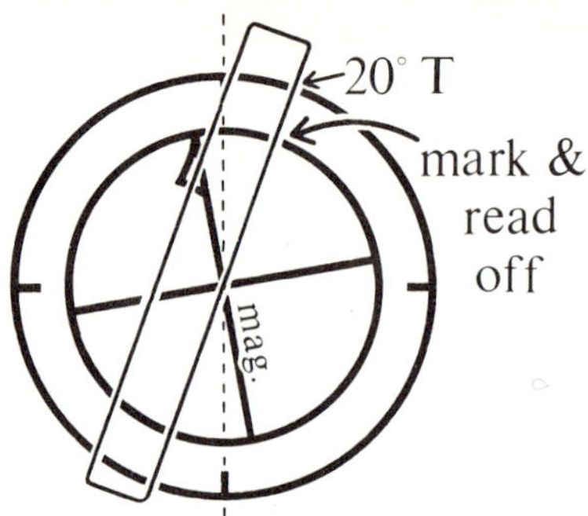

Figure 5. *Converting a bearing on the compass rose.*

edge cuts the magnetic rose and read off the magnetic bearing. *Don't* attempt, by use of mnemonics or otherwise, to correct bearings by calculation. If you make a mistake and do it the wrong way round, you have a 20–25° difference; despite what may be said about errors in Chapter 7, this is not the kind of mistake you can afford to live with!

Depth and height information

We have already touched on soundings and heights. Now that charts have gone metric, *you should work entirely in metres* (just as you should work entirely on magnetic bearings), but during the transition period you will want to convert from feet and fathoms (1 fathom = 6 feet) to metres. There are handy three-way conversion scales (looking like ladders) on most Admiralty charts, and *Reed's* contains comprehensive conversion tables (Section XVII).

Metric Admiralty charts are *layer-tinted*, and this is a tremendous help to the amateur navigator, especially when conditions are difficult.

Safe water (over 5 m chart datum depth) is WHITE.
Shallow water (5 m – 0 datum) is BLUE.
The intertidal zone is GREEN, with *drying-out heights* underlined.
Land is YELLOW.

The tinting of the intertidal zone is particularly useful, as it was not always easy to see the line under a figure in a poor light in a heaving boat.

For further details of metric soundings and depth contours, see Sections Q and R of 5011.

Land features

Here one can do little more than recommend a study of Sections A–J of 5011, which correspond to the table of conventional signs on a map. Natural and artificial features selected as landmarks or as of other navigational interest, such as port facilities, are clearly and accurately marked and well described, but other features which may be quite conspicuous to the eye are often only vaguely indicated. It is important to remember that built-up areas are shown only by a fine outline; they are not hatched or coloured dark as they are on most maps (see I 1, 3 and 3a of 5011).

You should also bear in mind that when the appearance of a natural or artificial feature is described on a chart or in sailing directions its designation, say as 'conspicuous', may only apply when it is seen from the bearing or sector of greatest navigational significance. Bawdsey Manor, for instance, which marks the entrance to the River Deben in Suffolk, is an unmistakable and impressive pile when seen from anywhere west of South, but nestles on a wooded slope and is almost invisible as you approach along the coast from the north east. Light and particularly mist can play strange tricks too; I must confess to having confused the Barfleur and Cap de la Hague lighthouses (at the east and west extremities of the Contentin Peninsula) one misty dawn. In fact we set course for Cherbourg across the Seine Bay (i.e. away from it) and only discovered our error when we took a radio fix.

We shall be discussing the practical and psychological problems of landfalls in Chapter 9. Suffice it to say here that the better you know a stretch of coast, the more difficult it often seems to identify its features correctly as you close it. Medium-scale Admiralty charts covering coasts where landfalls are frequently made often have a *shore profile* (usually along the bottom edge). These profiles are invaluable, the more so if the navigator remembers to consult and memorize them in advance before the arguments start! For instance, one would never think that, approached from the South, the Isle of Wight between St Catherine's Point and the Needles looks like two large headlands with a broad, deep bay in between – until of course you get close enough to see the ground near sea level.

Dangers and restrictions (Sections O and P of 5011)

You must learn Serials 1–4 of Section O (for metric charts); the rules for colouring and notation of heights are as already described. Note however the symbol for a rock awash at chart datum; this is an easy (disastrous!) one to overlook. Dangerous tide conditions (Serials 18 and 19) are discussed in Chapter 6. The most important symbols in Section P are Serials 1, 2 and 5 (Chapters 4, 8 and 19), 4 (Chapter 4), 12 and 21.

Building up a picture

By now you will have appreciated the vast amount of detail that Admiralty charts contain and will have begun to form an idea of the elements in this section which are directly or indirectly of importance to you. As you become familiar with charts, you will begin to find them interesting and often aesthetically pleasing. Studying them closely will become a pleasure rather than a chore. This is the point at which you really start to use charts properly and to build up a comprehensive mental image from poring over them. It is useful to make up your lists of marks and lights (see page 66) from the chart and recheck them in the books rather than vice versa; this forces you to concentrate on chart detail. Don't reject information just because it seems irrelevant. You may look at a rock or shoal when you are planning and think it need not worry you. Then you have to beat, or you are late and have to stand right in to plug a tide. You will be tired and conditions may be bad. It is then that the odd bits of information which the good navigator pulls out of the chart and tucks away in his mind start to matter.

But in poring over a familiar chart don't forget the need for it to be up-to-date – and bear in mind that even the most recent information may have been overtaken by events.

4

Marks, Lights and Sound Signals

REFERENCES: *Symbols and Abbreviations used in Admiralty Charts*, Ref. 5011, Sections K, L, L70, M, N; *Admiralty Lists of Lights and Fog Signals*, Vol. A, British Isles and North Coast of France (Hydrographer of the Navy, NR 74); *Reed's Nautical Almanac* – frontispiece, Sections XXVI and XXVII and Port Index; RYA Seamanship Foundation poster on IALA buoyage; any convenient medium-scale Admiralty chart (metric, IALA buoyage).

Modern yachtsmen are so used to sailing excellently marked and charted waters that they take marks for granted and would probably – and doubtless wisely – be unwilling to enter any unmarked coastal or inland waters, especially at night. Since however the marks are mainly designed for commercial shipping, there remains much scope for pilotage skills in deciding what is and is not possible for a yacht, in picking the best course, and in choosing which marks and/or lights to work from in a given situation.

Marks do much more than indicate position or where it is and is not safe to go. Used in conjunction with charts they, like charts themselves, offer the trained eye – and in this case the trained ear too – a mass of information. Before plunging into detail, it may be worth having a general look at the means by which this information is conveyed. Beacons apart, marks have a *body*, and this will have a characteristic colour, shape and size, any or all of which may serve simply to distinguish it or may have a specific meaning. In addition buoys have their *name* painted on the surface or on a plate attached to their structure. Beacons, and now most buoys, have a *topmark*; in addition to its visual characteristics of colour, shape and size, this will usually be designed to give a clear radar response, sometimes one that will allow identification of its shape.

Navigational lights are distinguishable from shore lights by being intermittent and/or coloured – never white and constant ('fixed'). Their characteristics are colour, pattern of flashes (character), timing (period) and under some circumstances brightness. Lights on buoys are normally located on top of the body, but certain buoys, rather confusingly described as 'high focal plane', are of greater than normal height with the light fitted near the level of the topmark.

Sound signals are characterized by the type of sound (horn, bell, etc.) and again by character and period. Thus:

Day		*Night*		*Fog*	
Body and/or topmark	colour shape size	Light	colour character period	Sound	type character period
Topmark		Radar response			

So we see that a mark may have as many as ten characteristics which the navigator must be able to decode from the entries in his books and on his charts, and to recognize by eye or ear. In addition to this the *set* of a buoy, that is the angle and direction in which it is tilted, and its *wake*, give an excellent idea of strength and direction of tidal stream (Chapter 6).

Lights (5011, Sections K and L70, Introduction to *List of Lights*)

Now that there is an even closer association than there used to be between types of buoy and the characteristics of their lights, it may be helpful to discuss lights first.

Colour

Violet, orange or blue lights may be used in special cases, especially where there is any risk of confusion with shore lights or visual beacons for aircraft, but the lights of navigational marks are normally of one of four colours. Three of these (red, green and yellow) are the same as the main colour of the buoy that carries them, and primarily black buoys have white lights (see below).

Class and character

A light which appears uninterrupted to an observer stationary in relation to it is known as a *fixed light*. Lights of the fixed class are *never* white (nor, so far as I know, yellow, orange or blue and thus liable to be confused with sodium or mercury vapour shore lights). Fixed coloured lights are mainly used to demarcate shorelines and their features, thus roughly corresponding to beacons.

All white lights and most coloured ones are *rhythmic*; they light up intermittently according to a specific cycle of operations. The proportion of time for which they are lit and unlit is the first element in their *character*; the possibilities are:

1. FLASHING (Fl): longer unlit than lit.
2. ISOPHASE (Iso): equal lit and unlit, alternating evenly.
3. OCCULTING (Occ): actually or at least apparently longer lit than unlit (although total duration of light and eclipse may be equal).

For the first and third of these, three kinds of variation are possible, namely *rate* of flashing, *grouping* of flashes and *period*, the time taken for a complete cycle. On rate we can distinguish:

Very quick flash (VQkFl)	2 flashes per second
Quick flash (QkFl)	1 flash per second
Interrupted quick flash (IntQkFl) Group flash (GpFl)	1 flash per second (when flashing)
Flash (Fl)	1 flash per period
Long flash (LFl)	a flash lasting at least 2 seconds

Occulting (Occ) and *Group Occulting* (GpOcc) are the converse of Flashing and Group Flashing. Other variations of the *Rhythmic Class* and detail of the *Alternating Class* of lights are set out in the Introductory Remarks to the *Admiralty List of Lights*. Briefly, alternating lights may be of one of three kinds:

1. Continuous light with changes of *colour* on same bearing.
2. Fixed lights with a flash or group flash of greater brilliance superimposed.
3. Lights whose overall period contains two distinct characters.

One of the most common reasons for failing to identify lights or mixing them up is misunderstanding the term *period*, particularly in the case of group flashing or occulting lights. The period is that of the complete cycle, *not* the interval between one group of flashes and the next (Figure 6).

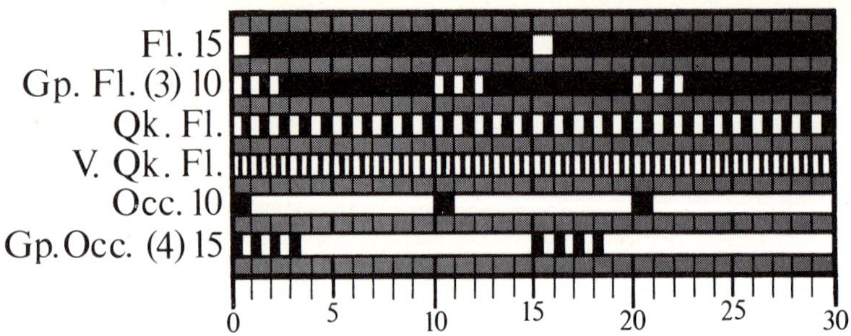

Figure 6. *Typical rhythmic light characters.*

Sector lights

Many lighthouses and some buoys show different coloured lights in different sectors (Figure 7). Generally speaking the central sector will be WHITE; subject to any other local dangers, marked or otherwise, a ship in the white sector is in safe waters or is closing on the correct approach. The RED sector is placed relative to the white so that a ship closing the light in the white sector and changing course or being swept to port will see the red; it is thus equivalent to a *port-hand* marker. Conversely the GREEN sector is usually equivalent to a *starboard-hand* marker. Lights on a point running across a harbour mouth may have *two white sectors.* In this case the red and green sectors will correspond to the buoyage convention for the side they are seen, i.e. a ship leaving harbour will see *red* to *starboard.* A light on a stretch of coast may sometimes comply with the coastwise buoyage convention (see below) and show two green or red sectors, one on either side of the white.

Range and loom

The range at which a light can be seen may be limited by its brightness (luminous range) or, in good visibility, by the horizon (geographical range). *Nominal luminous range* is based on 10 nm visibility. When a powerful light is below the horizon, its loom may be seen. This is a vague and rather faint representation of the light but is usually good enough to identify the character of the light or to steer on it. The distance off at which loom changes to light proper (known as the *dipping range*) can be found by using the appropriate table in *Reed's* (Table II – To Find Distance off Lights Rising or Dipping, in *Section VII*, 'Coastal Passage Making').

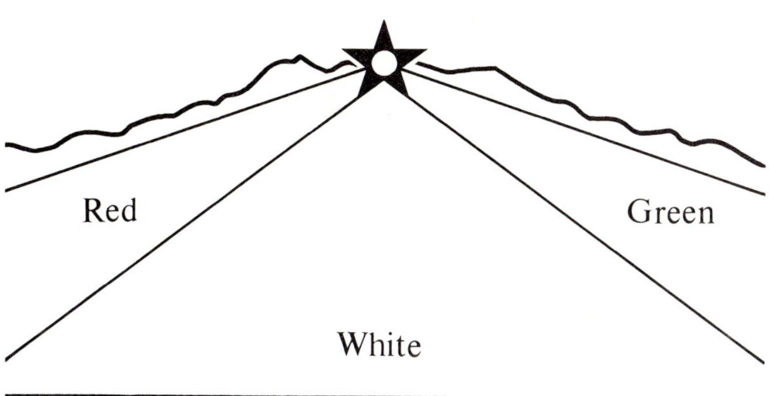

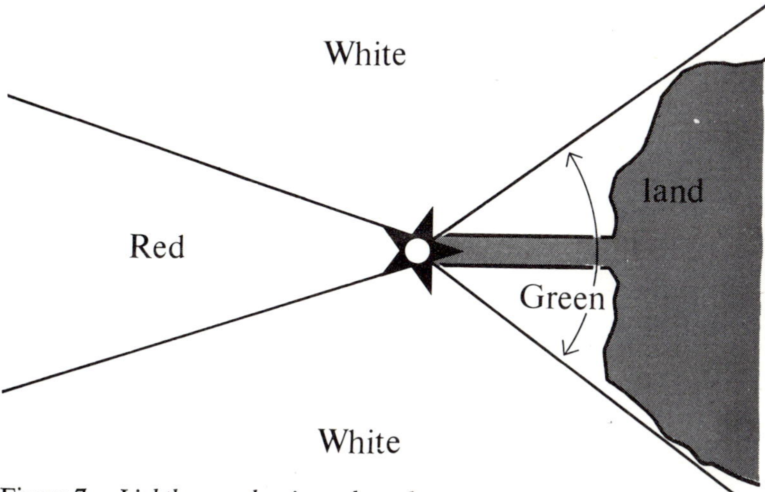

Figure 7. *Lighthouses showing coloured sectors.*

Navigational sound signals (5011, Section N)

It is important to distinguish sound signals on navigational marks, generally known as *fog signals*, from sound signals used by shipping both in clear weather and in fog. As the Fathoms Charts and Metric Charts tables of Section N of 5011 show, the number of 'patent' types of fog signal is tending to diminish. *Bell*, *whistle*, *reed* and *gong* speak for themselves.

A reed is a rather feeble sound, pitched below a whistle but well above the other sustained types of signal. The *diaphone*'s sound is rather powerful, low-pitched and characterized by a short sound of lower pitch known as the 'grunt' (usually at the end of the blast). *Sirens* use compressed air and tend to be of medium and sometimes variable pitch. *Horns* come in many types; basically they use a diaphragm and thus give a rather more 'positive' sound than the other types of signal. Pitch is usually low and may be steady or variable; some horn units, particularly the more powerful, have two pitches, giving a chord – in fact more often a discord!

The IALA 'A' buoyage system (Figure 8; pages 58–59)

REFERENCES: 5011 L70; frontispiece to *Reed's*; and RYA poster.

Up to 1977 each country had its own buoyage system; although these had many features in common, there were a number of important and confusing differences. The International Association of Lighthouse Authorities (IALA) finally reached agreement on the standard system for European waters, and this is being introduced under a five-year programme, stage one of which was implemented in 1977. I shall confine discussion to the IALA 'A' system. The British lateral system is fully covered in *Reed's*, and other northern European systems are sufficiently described there and in Barbara Webb's *Dictionary* (see page 18); once again 5011, Section L, is an invaluable source.

First however it is worth considering briefly the purpose of buoys and what they mean to the yachtsman. Most buoys demarcate the boundary between safe and unsafe waters; they may enclose a shoal in the middle of a passage or indicate the safe distance offshore. Sometimes they show the middle of a channel, serving as a mark to steer on. A single buoy may be used to mark an isolated danger such as a submerged rock; and yet other buoys, which are not navigation marks in the true sense, indicate special features. You will thus see that buoys tell you nothing unless you are familiar with their code and more particularly unless you *use them in conjunction with an up-to-date chart.* At the simplest you will not otherwise know how closely you can approach a buoy.

But what buoys in fact do is to tell you your position on the chart and allow you to follow the course you want without resort, or at least with only minimal resort, to position-finding techniques. Whether you are in a buoyed area or not, the *chart* remains your basic tool. If you are running down the coast to enter a major port there is no point in standing out to round the outermost channel marker if a boat of your draught can safely cut into the channel a mile or two nearer shore – and this the chart will tell you.

Direction of buoyage

The same set of buoys has to cater for ships moving in both directions, so that there has to be a conventional *direction of buoyage.* Ships moving in the direction of buoyage treat starboard-hand marks as such, passing to port of them; ships moving against it treat starboard-hand marks as if they were port-hand marks and pass to starboard of them (Figure 9). In all systems, the direction of buoyage is away from the sea in entrance channels, harbours and inland waterways; the buoys lead you *in.* This direction is perpendicular to the coast; a second direction has to be established parallel to the

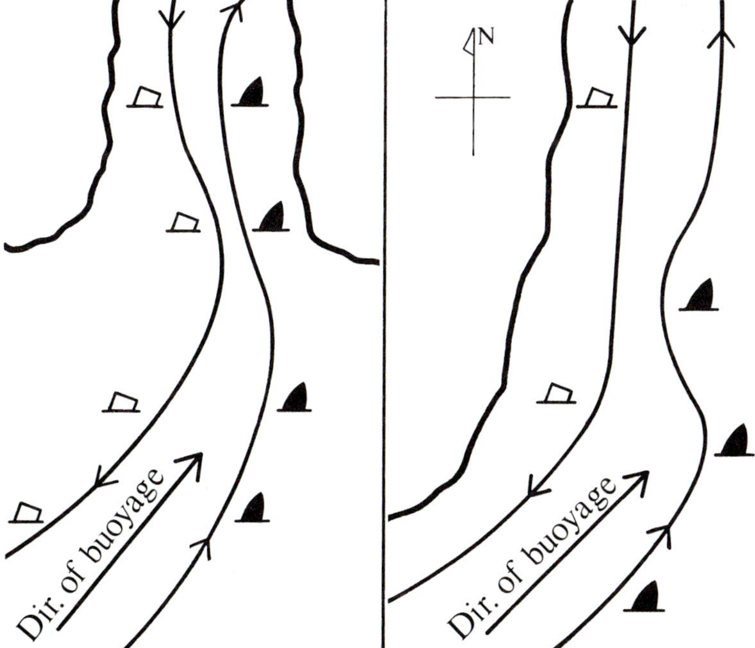

Figure 9. *Direction of buoyage.*

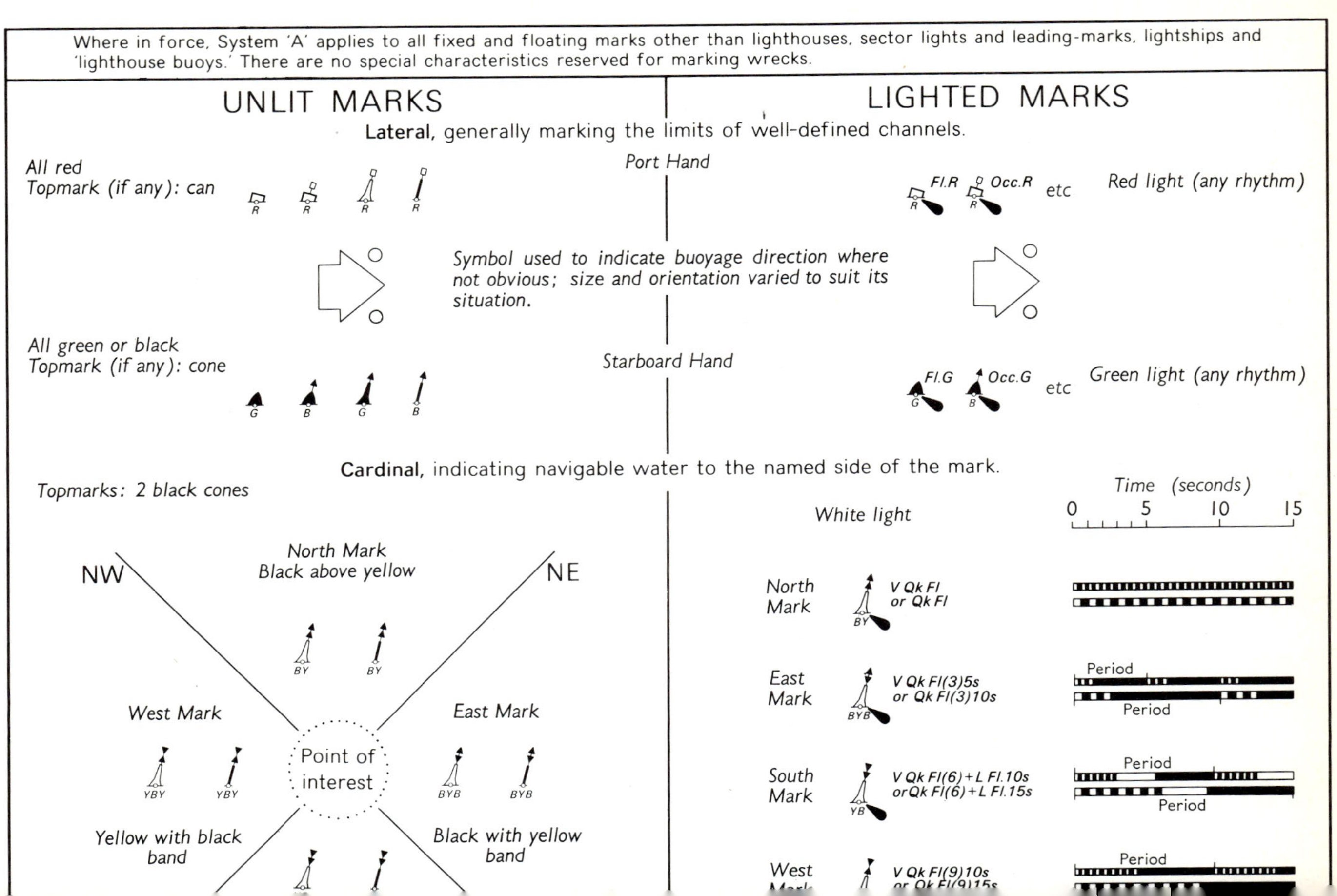
Where in force, System 'A' applies to all fixed and floating marks other than lighthouses, sector lights and leading-marks, lightships and 'lighthouse buoys.' There are no special characteristics reserved for marking wrecks.
UNLIT MARKS
LIGHTED MARKS
Lateral, generally marking the limits of well-defined channels.
All red
Topmark (if any): can
R
Port Hand
Fl.R
Occ.R
etc
Red light (any rhythm)
Symbol used to indicate buoyage direction where not obvious; size and orientation varied to suit its situation.
All green or black
Topmark (if any): cone
G
B
Starboard Hand
Fl.G
Occ.G
etc
Green light (any rhythm)
Cardinal, indicating navigable water to the named side of the mark.
Topmarks: 2 black cones
North Mark
Black above yellow
NW
NE
BY
West Mark
YBY
Point of interest
East Mark
BYB
Yellow with black band
Black with yellow band
White light
Time (seconds)
0
5
10
15
North Mark
V Qk Fl
or Qk Fl
East Mark
V Qk Fl(3)5s
or Qk Fl(3)10s
Period
South Mark
V Qk Fl(6)+L Fl.10s
orQk Fl(6)+L Fl.15s
YB
West
V Qk Fl(9)10s

The very quick flash or quick flash grouping of the lights conforms to the clock face. Thus:

Cardinal point of SAFE *side*	*Body colour*	*Topmark (all black)*	*Light (all white)*
North	black over yellow	2 cones, points up	very quick or quick flash (uninterrupted)
South	yellow over black	2 cones, points down	very quick group flash 6 + long flash every 10 secs *or* quick group flash 6 + long flash every 15 secs
East	black yellow black	2 cones, points outwards	very quick group flash 3 every 5 secs *or* quick group flash 3 every 10 secs
West	yellow black yellow	2 cones, points inwards	very quick group flash 9 every 10 secs *or* quick group flash 9 every 15 secs

The third class of IALA marks subdivides into three types.

Isolated danger marks are used to indicate a small isolated danger with safe water all round, such as a submerged wreck or rock. They are pillars or spars coloured black with one or more red bands. (By definition 'bands' are horizontal, 'stripes' are vertical.) Their topmarks are two black spheres, and their lights white group flash 2.

Safe-water marks indicate mid-channel or safe landfall points. They are spheres with red and white stripes. They may have a single red sphere as topmark; their lights are white and may be isophase, occulting or one long flash every 10 seconds.

Special marks are used for any other purpose; their significance can be seen from the chart. They are coloured yellow and their topmarks (if any) are a single yellow X. Shape is not specified, but 'may not conflict with navigational marks'; despite this, cones with a topmark seem to be favoured. Lights are yellow, of a rhythm distinct from that of the IALA white navigational lights.

I foresee three problems for amateur navigators, all in connection with the cardinal marks. The first is that the type of buoy shows the *direction of safe water*, not of the hazard. The second is that you have to know roughly where north is all the time. And the third is that, despite the mnemonic and the clock-face light rhythm, it is very easy to confuse east and west.

Leading marks and lights, transits (5011, Sections K and P)

Leading marks and lights are a pair of marks on which you align and towards which you steer until you reach a point where some further instruction applies (Figure 10). This is one form of transit. Other forms of transit are two marks straddling the boat, and two marks astern. Thus leading marks for entering habour become transit marks for leaving it. Or a transit may be formed by a channel marker or safe-water buoy and a mark or feature on land (see also pages 98–9).

Leading and transit lights always have the characteristics of navigational lights, that is they are always coloured and/or rhythmic or alternating. Daylight marks may be either special beacons, often incorporating the equivalent lights, or natural or artificial features such as a nick in a cliff-line or a church spire. In addition, the chart or sailing directions may indicate a single conspicuous feature, such as the big block of flats at Cherbourg, for which you head until you see the entrance itself. A pair of leading marks or a transit gives you direction as well as a point to steer on; a single mark must of course be used in conjunction with a bearing or sector.

Descriptions of marks and lights

Details of marks and lights are given in abbreviated form. You must be able to decode these in whichever source you first look them up, and to compare them in your other sources for purposes of double checking and to complete the information. This information is given on Admiralty charts, as well as in *Reed's* and the *Admiralty List of Lights*. The information given on charts is explained in 5011; *Reed's* has an explanation at the beginning of Section XXVI immediately followed by a table of abbreviations and characteristics. The abbreviations used in the *Admiralty List of Lights* are explained right at the beginning (pages 6 and 7 in the current edition of Volume A).

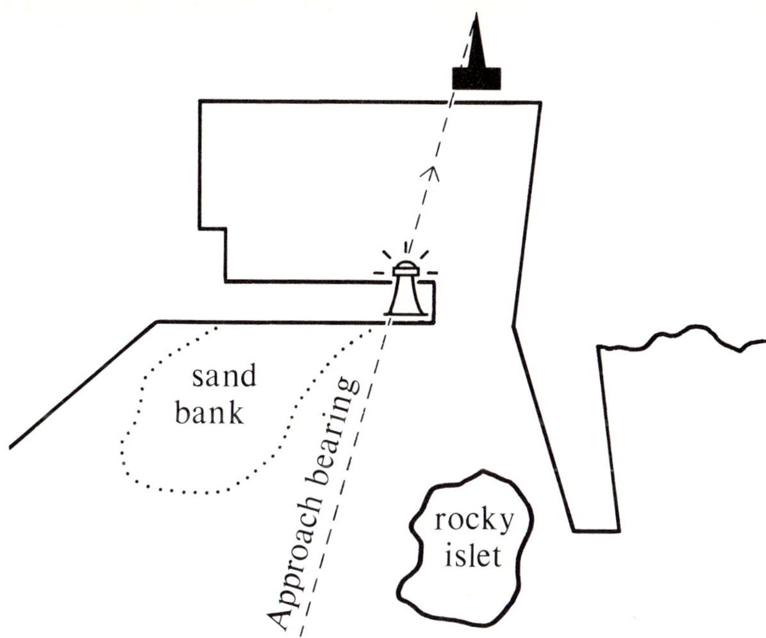

Figure 10. *Leading marks/lights.*

The best way to familiarize yourself with all this detail is to take two or three major buoys and lighthouses in your home waters, look them up in all three sources and compose a full description of them using every bit of information given. You can then check this description physically to see whether you have interpreted it correctly (see also page 66).

Verbal indication of marks

You need some simple and certain method of communicating the position of marks – and of shipping, topographical features, etc. – between crew members. The navigator may need to indicate a mark to the helmsman, or someone who has spotted a mark may want to draw the navigator's attention to it. By day traditional descriptions such as 'fine on the port bow' or 'through the starboard shrouds' may suffice, as long as all concerned appreciate the effects of parallax (Figure 11). What A sees as on the bow, B sees as 'through the port shrouds'. At night something rather more systematic is needed; I personally prefer the method of 180° sectors (Figure 12). The sector

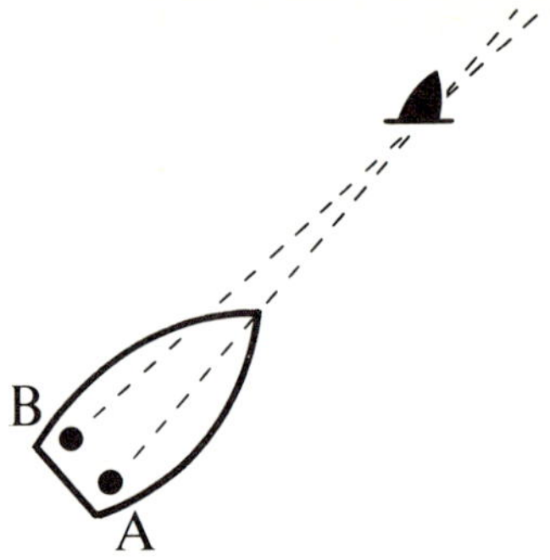

Figure 11. *Parallax effect and observed angle.*

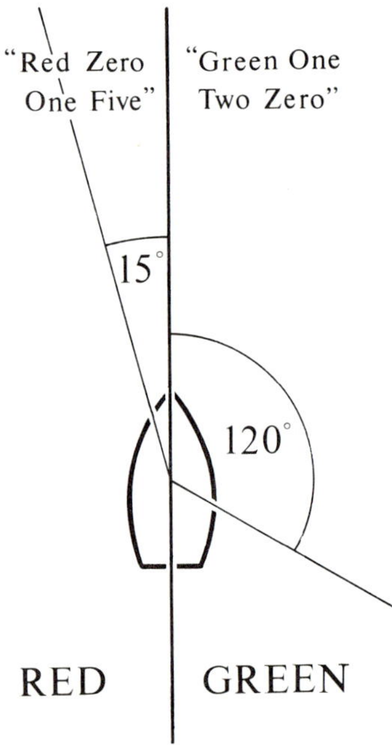

Figure 12. *Indication of angles off head.*

to starboard of the boat's axis is called GREEN (matching navigation light and channel markers) and the port sector RED. Angle is estimated off the bow, figures being given digit by digit, e.g. RED ZERO ONE FIVE, GREEN ONE TWO ZERO.

Counting of lights

You must be able to identify the period of a light fairly accurately. Remember that the period is the *whole cycle* (see page 53). Some people can count seconds fairly accurately (I must confess to using the 'hippopotamus' method), but if there is any doubt and particularly if your preparations have disclosed two lights with similar characteristics you must confirm by stop-watch. You must count the number of flashes in a group at least three times while keeping the light continuously under observation, and it is best to get a second person to check it in the same way. Be particularly careful in heavy seas, when a distant light or one low down on a buoy may be visible only intermittently.

Distinguishing shore and navigational lights

It is sometimes extremely difficult to distinguish shore and navigational lights, as bright shore lighting tends to blot out navigational lights in line with it. A well-known example of this problem is heading east through the Solent and trying to find the 'hole in the wall' against the lights of Southsea. But no port backed or flanked by a town with modern lighting is easy to see your way into, and entrances near brilliantly lit port installations are particularly tricky. The navigator and as many other crew members as possible must memorize what lights they are looking for and their approximate and relative position. Once you pick up one navigational light, you can then normally use it to locate the others.

The following point may seem absurd, but it is a very good example of the way in which a mixture of fatigue, confusion and an element of fear can blur both observation and judgement. The headlights of a car passing through undulating country or going down a twisty road, or those of a series of cars going down a stretch of road or street, can give the impression of a flashing or occulting light. If you happen to be searching for a light of roughly similar character against a blaze of shore lights, the sight of an apparently rhythmic light may lead you to very dangerous conclusions. The other dangerous effect of shore lights is that they destroy night adaptation of the retina and thus make it difficult to see unlit objects in the water; this however is a problem of seamanship rather than navigation.

Listing marks for a passage

This chapter, and particularly the short sections immediately above, will I hope have driven home the need for good homework. As part of the preparation for a passage, especially if part of it is or may be by night, you must familiarize yourself with *every light and mark* you may see and make a list for quick reference. I in fact like to use two lists: one of the marks I intend to work from; and another of those which may confuse me or which I may need if I have to beat or get off my planned course for any other reason.

5

Tide Heights and Depths

REFERENCE: *Reed's Nautical Almanac.*

To the yachtsman tide is second in importance only to wind; to the yachtsman in many north European waters it probably ranks above wind both as a means of going where he wants and as a source of difficulty and danger. There are two quite distinct effects of tide. One is its rise and fall, which affects the depth of water at any given moment; the other, more complex and usually even more important, is a horizontal one, the tidal stream. We shall look at rise and fall in this chapter and tackle tidal stream separately in the next. (For a fuller explanation of tides and tidal effects, see Section XIV of *Reed's*.)

Springs and neaps

Tides are caused by the gravitational pull of the moon and the sun; the strength of this pull will depend on the relative positions of earth, moon and sun and the distances between these bodies. Tide heights follow a fortnightly cycle, on which are superimposed less important monthly and six-monthly cycles. The *range* of a tide is the difference in level between a high water and the preceding low water. Theoretically the range will be greatest at new moon and full moon, but in fact there is a lag of some forty-eight hours in European waters, so that *spring tides* (nothing to do with the season!) occur about two days after new and full moon. The tides of least range, known as neaps, occur about two days after the first and third quarters of the moon. Each monthly cycle of the moon will produce one major and one minor spring tide, and the highest springs of the year will tend to occur around or just after the equinoxes (March and September).

This is the basis on which tide tables are compiled, but *weather* can produce variations. An onshore wind and low barometric pressure tend to increase sea level, and an offshore wind and high pressure to lower it. In addition certain areas are subject to considerably more pronounced effects. A persistent strong or even moderate wind blowing in the same direction as the tidal stream may cause as much as one metre difference in rise and fall, amounting to forty or fifty per cent of the predicted range at some places where this is small. (For example a difference of 730 mm from predicted range was recorded at Lowestoft early in June 1977.) The meteorological effect on the strength of the tidal stream (Chapter 6) is similar to that on its duration but more marked, producing extreme local and temporary variations. (The author observed an increase approaching 100 per cent in April 1977 off Sizewell on the East coast.) These *storm surges* are normally followed by a reaction, and several fluctuations may occur before things return to normal. Storm surges are most common and best known in the Southern North Sea, but a growing body of evidence suggests that they occur over any long stretch of coast along which the prevailing winds are parallel to the tidal streams.

There is a convention that extends the terms 'flood' and 'ebb' to coastwise tidal streams. This probably grew up by association with the pre-IALA conventions on direction of coastwise buoyage (see page 57), which took the Thames estuary and the Solway Firth as 'upstream'. Expert opinion has always been against this extended use of 'flood' and 'ebb', and the new direction of buoyage makes it extremely confusing.

This is a convenient point at which to sum up the states of the tide recognized and used in navigational documentation; they are tabulated from highest level to lowest (see table on facing page).

Finding times and heights of high and low water, and depths

Section XIV of *Reed's Nautical Almanac* contains three major types of table:

1. High and low water at major standard ports, e.g. Dover.
2. High water at other standard ports, e.g. Harwich.

3. Tidal differences of secondary ports with respect to standard ports, e.g. Brightlingsea/Harwich.

Note that the first two kinds of table, like nearly all nautical documentation, give *all times in GMT (ZULU time)*. The Dover table occupies three pages, giving date, day of week, and times and heights of high and low water. Note first, by comparing the equivalent entry for successive days, that there is a *daily time shift* of between 40 and 70 minutes, the greater shift tending to occur around neaps; a good yardstick figure is *50 minutes*. Then study successive *high water levels* to get an impression of the pattern of *springs and neaps*. Then compare these in succession with the corresponding *low water levels*, to get a feel for *ranges* and their variations. You will also see from the footnote that heights are referred to Lowest Astronomical Tide. Having found the time you want, don't forget to correct it!

The second type of table, occupying two pages, gives high water times and heights only. If you need low water times and/or heights, you use the Tidal Difference tables. To find the approximate time of low water, *6¼ hours after high water* is a good yardstick figure. For greater accuracy you must refer to the Tidal Difference table concerned. Suppose for instance we find that afternoon high water at Harwich on 10 May 1977 is 1710 Z (GMT) = 1810 A (BST) and the height is 3·6 m. Now look at the table, Tidal Differences on Harwich, and the line for Harwich. The centre column shows *Duration of*

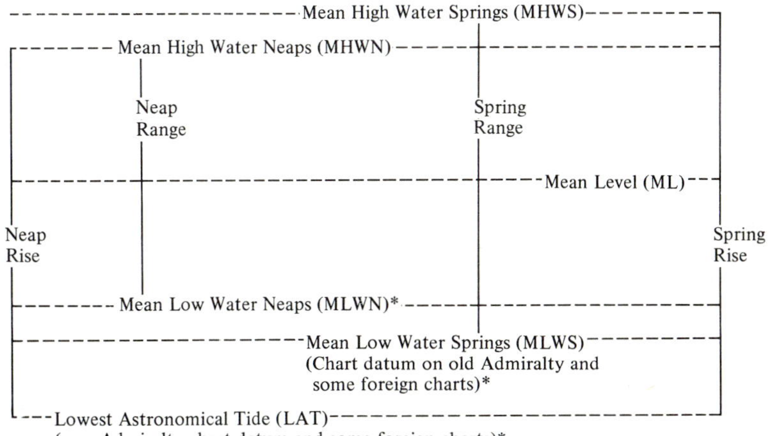

*Chart datum levels used by various countries range from Mean Low Water to 'lowest possible tide' (France).

Mean Rise (DMR), in this case 6 hrs 30 min. By subtracting the DMR from the time of high water we get a fairly accurate time for low water – in this case 1810 – 6 hrs 30 = 1140 A. To find the *depth* at Harwich Outer Pier at high water, add the tide height to the chart datum depth (CD, last column), 5·5 + 3·6 = 9·1 m. To find the *height of low water* we use the Mean Level (ML) column. Double the ML figure and *subtract from this* the height at high water to give the *height at low water*, 2·2 × 2 – 3·6 = +0·8 m. We can now find the *range*, 3·6 – 0·8 = 2·8 m. However a quicker way of finding range if low water height is not known is: *range is twice the difference between HW height and mean level, R = 2(HW Ht – ML).* By adding this low water height to the chart datum sounding we get *low water depth*, 5·5 + 0·8 = 6·3 m.

Next let us find the complete information for Manningtree Quay, again using the table, Tidal Differences on Harwich. Note that, having found our base figure in A time (BST), we continue to work in that time.

High water time:
  1810 A (Harwich) + 30 mins (column 1, MHW, Tm. Diff.) = 1840A
High water height:
  3·6 m (Harwich) + 0·2 m (column 2, MHW, Ht Diff.) = 3·8 m
Low water time:
  1840A – 5 hrs 40 (column 4, DMR) = 1300 hrs
Low water height:
  2 × 2·3 (column 3, ML) – 3·8 (HWHt) = 0·6 m
Range:
  3·8 m (HWHt) – 0·6 m (LWHt) = 3·2 m
Low water depth:
  (– 1·0) (last column, CD) + 0·6 = – 0·4 m, *i.e. dries 0·4 m*

A negative answer to low water depth means that the point in question dries out!

Finding intermediate heights from tide range

To find the height of the tide at any given moment between high and low water, you must first establish the *range* in one of the ways described above. Imagine for a moment that you are ashore and drive from your house to the pub along a straight, unobstructed village street and back; you start from rest, gather speed, slow down and stop – and the same on the way home. This is just what happens with tidal flow, so simply dividing the range by 6 or 6·5 (hours) will not give you an accurate enough result, accurate enough, that is, if you are in a position where you need to worry about depth at all.

You therefore use the *rule of twelve*; the mnemonic I use for this is: 'In the waltz, do you reverse?', i.e. 1, 2, 3 – 3, 2, 1; but younger readers may be able to invent something more to their taste. The rise or fall will be 1/12 in the first and last hours, 2/12 in the second and fifth and 3/12 in the two middle ones. Divide the range by *12*; in our example for Harwich, 2·8 m ÷ 12 is near enough 0·23 m – or to help you visualize it – 9 inches. So starting from low water (1140 A), we can tabulate heights through to the next high water.

1140 A		= 0·8 m
1240 A	0·8 + *1* × 0·23	= 1·03 m
1340 A	1·03 + *2* × 0·23	= 1·49 m
1440 A	1·49 + *3* × 0·23	= 2·18 m
1540 A	2·18 + *3* × 0·23	= 2·87 m
1640 A	2·87 + *2* × 0·23	= 3·33 m
1740 A	3·33 + *1* × 0·23	= 3·56 m

rising to 3·6 m by the actual time of high water, 1810 A. Similarly we can work downwards:

1810 A		= 3·6 m
1910 A	3·6 – *1* × 0·23	= 3·37 m
....		
2310 A	3·6 – (1 + 2 + 3 + 3 + 2 = 11) × 0·23	= 1·07 m
0040 A (11 May)	3·6 – 12 × 0·23	= 0·84 m

Note that you can jump straight to any particular hour provided you get the number of twelfths right.

If you now use methods you have already learnt to check this for the next tide, you will find that you never come out exactly right on height or time. This is because the rule of twelve is an approximation; the errors caused by it are however no greater than the differences to be expected between predicted and actual times and heights. So, as we shall see in Chapter 7, we can very easily live with this kind of error.

At this point you might do well to rework this and the preceding section using standard and secondary ports in waters you know.

Depths above chart datum

Once you have found the tide height hour by hour, or for any particular time you are interested in, you can calculate and tabulate any local depths you need to know by adding this to the chart datum figure:

Tide height PLUS sounding = depth.
Tide height MINUS drying height = depth.

Remember that the intertidal zone is tinted green, and drying heights have the unit figure underlined (see pages 46 and 48).

It is well worth preparing a table of this kind before a passage if you are proposing to take a short cut over a bank, to stand right in because of tidal streams (Chapter 6), or most of all to enter harbour over a shallow bar (Chapter 19).

Checking reference depths and calibrating echo-sounder

Even where you are not expecting conditions critical enough to justify the rather tedious procedures described above, *you must have a key figure in your mind from which you can mentally estimate tide height, and you must check this against your echo-sounder*. Look at the large- or medium-scale chart you are using to leave harbour and pick a sounding or two over which you can guide the helmsman precisely. Work out the tide heights for these at the time you expect to pass over them, which at that stage you can predict with some certainty. Check your calculation against the echo-sounder reading, not forgetting the possibility of false readings and the fact that the transducer of your echo-sounder is a certain distance below the waterline (see page 39). If your calculation and the sounding roughly agree, fine; if not, do a new calculation and recheck over another convenient point. This will serve both to prove your key figure and to fix it in your mind. You will of course have to correct it mentally for rise and fall of tide as time passes. You are then in a position to use the echo-sounder with confidence to check whether you have enough water under you (Chapters 8 and 19) and as an aid to position-finding (see page 138).

There is a kind of eleventh commandment about navigating in marginal depths. Going where you safely can but big ships cannot is a good safety measure and the mark of a competent navigator who knows the waters and/or has done his homework. Going aground, on the other hand, is a black mark, although a frequent enough one. You thus need to stay firmly but not excessively on the safe side of the composite error zone of chart data, tide predictions and echo-sounder readings. As we shall see in Chapters 8 and 19, if you are going to do something which carries a risk of running aground, *do it as early as possible on the flood with the tide moving from neaps to springs.*

6
Tidal Streams

REFERENCES: Hydrographer of the Navy (Pocket) Tidal Stream Atlas for your home waters; *Reed's Nautical Almanac*; *Symbols and Abbreviations used on Admiralty Charts* (Hydrographer of the Navy, Chart No. 5011); any medium-scale metric Admiralty chart with tidal stream table and marks; any map or chart of the central part of the English Channel.

The pattern of rise and fall of tides means that water is transferred from one geographical location to another; in other words it flows. It is conventional to talk of the flow of water into and out of a harbour or tidal river as a 'tide' and of coastwise and offshore flows as 'tidal streams', but this distinction is at best one of scale. Many yachtsmen seem to have little idea of the significance of tidal streams, and even those experienced in tidal waters often underestimate their importance. The lesson was brought home to me by watching fishing fleets of junks in the waters round Hong Kong. It is difficult to make many designs of fishing junk go to windward, and I was puzzled how the fleet got where it wanted to be. There is a rather complex pattern of reverse currents in these waters; when it is calm you can see the tide rips clearly. In effect the fishing boats used their sails simply to get into and stay in the tidal stream they wanted; one could see them 'changing trains' so to speak.

This reminiscence serves to bring out the first point about tidal streams. However your boat is moving relative to the water, the water itself is moving relative to the land, just as if your boat was in a vast tank being transported along a road or railway. There is nothing you can do about this; the discipline of the tides and more particularly of tidal streams is one to which you must submit.

Second, *the speed of tidal streams is of the same order as the speed of a yacht*. For example the Froude formula speed of a 6·5 m LWL displacement monohull would be rather under 6 k. In some areas we find predicted tidal streams of 6 k and more, and in others meteorological conditions may greatly increase quoted stream strengths of around 3 k (see page 68). Even larger racing yachts may encounter tidal streams of over 50 per cent of their best speed. Thus tide is just as important as wind in getting a boat from A to B and is a fundamental factor in navigation and passage planning.

An admittedly extreme example may serve to bring this point home; it is the passage of 80–90 nm. or so from Cherbourg to St Malo at springs. There is an inshore reverse current (described by Adlard Coles) from the Cherbourg entrance round to Carteret during the last two to three hours of the main east-going stream; this adds up to maybe 4 nm.s' worth and puts you at the top of the Alderney Race when the stream turns. Thence the south-west stream will give you about 27 nm., so that you have had 31 nm. of tide under you. By that time you will have been sailing for about nine hours, say at 4 k, and covered about 35 nm. through the water. This makes rather over 65 miles in all which will put you off the south-west corner of the Minquiers, where the stream will by that time have turned and the flood tide will quarter you up until you turn into the St Malo entrance channel, giving you another 6 nm. or so. In this example, the tide will have given you just about 50 per cent of the distance made good and with luck you will have got to St Malo in ten or eleven hours' sailing and in time to lock through within an hour after high water. (If this example has 'lost' you, don't worry; passage planning is dealt with later.)

To conclude this introduction, I should like to offer the not entirely uninformed opinion that in some confined waters and estuaries tidal streams are tending to increase in strength and to become increasingly susceptible to the wind-over-tide effects already described.

Sources of tidal stream information

You will find a set of Tidal Stream Charts in *Reed's* (Section XIV) but I prefer to use the Admiralty Tidal Stream Atlases because their larger scale makes them easier to read and more particularly to mark up (see page 85). There is also a fair amount of information on local tidal stream effects in the Admiralty Pilots and much of direct interest to yachtsmen in unofficial sailing instructions and informative books. Like most other aspects of pilotage, it is a question of doing your homework thoroughly and building up the fullest picture you can. Since the tidal atlases for all waters round and near the British Isles are referred to *High Water Dover* even if a local secondary reference is quoted, I find it useful to keep the loose High Water Dover card provided with *Reed's* or the Admiralty card (*Time of High Water and Mean Range of Tide at Dover*, Hydrographer of the Navy, NP 164) in the tidal atlas I am using, particularly as these cards give *daily mean range*. *Reed's* card also illustrates range with a red line of varying length which shows at a glance just when the tide is making (increasing up to springs) or taking off (decreasing towards neaps).

Tidal atlases normally have thirteen hour-by-hour charts running from six hours before to six hours after High Water Dover. The length and thickness of the arrows serves to give a general impression of the tidal flow. The figures on each arrow or group of arrows are in *tenths of a knot*, so that 28 means 2·8 k. The figures are in pairs separated by a full-stop; the lower one is the neaps stream and the higher one is the springs stream. The inside front cover gives a table for computing intermediate values; this will be discussed below. To use it you must know the daily mean range (Chapter 5).

Last but not least among sources of tidal stream information is the chart (see page 46). Many medium-scale Admiralty charts give an hour-by-hour tidal stream table referred to specific points; these are indicated by a magenta diamond containing a key letter. The combined use of tidal atlas and chart is explained below.

Finding intermediate tidal stream figures

It is important to estimate how accurately you need to know the rates and local variations of tidal stream for a given passage under given conditions. Since tidal atlases are not updated between editions, there may be a basic error of 10–15 per cent compounded with a 'meteorological' error that, as we have seen above, may be considerably greater. If you have done your homework on tides properly so that you have a feel for the actual conditions, it is often enough to interpolate 'by eye'. This is a kind of adjusted averaging process which comes from experience. I suppose one first interpolates using high water levels as a guide and says: 'This is a half-way day', or 'a two-thirds-way day'; then one moves the figure up or down a bit depending on the relative directions of wind and tide, the set of a familiar buoy, the set or speed past the land of one's own boat and so on. Finally one rounds it to something manageable in one's head. I mention this approach because informed guesses, provided that they are reasonably well informed and completely honest, often give a truer answer than calculation.

The accurate method, a graphical one, is described in the Tidal Atlas and is very simple once you have found the *range* of the tide (pages 68–9 or the loose High Water Dover card). An even better way is to read the logged distance between two buoys or known points on the beam and subtract this from or add it to the measured distance (page 152). This will give you a reference figure for a particular hour from which you can calculate the rates for every hour of that tide. There are a number of similar methods based on comparing speed through the water and speed past the land, which will become obvious to you by the time you have finished this book.

Estimation of line of strongest/weakest stream

Let us first consider the question of 'catching the right train'. If you look at the Tidal Stream Charts for the Southern North Sea in *Reed's* (normally at the end of Section XIV) or, even better, at NP 251, the Admiralty Tidal Atlas for the North Sea (Southern portion), you will see that in the last three hours before High Water Dover the south-going stream divides about 'three arrows out' from Harwich. The inner stream turns into the Thames Estuary and the outer stream carries on south past the Kent coast into the Straits of Dover. If you are coming down from Lowestoft headed for Ramsgate or Calais, you need to place yourself to catch the outer stream, particularly as (see High Water Dover chart) you have slack a little way out while a foul tide is already belting round the North Foreland. Having got to a position east of Ramsgate, you then only have to cross the foul tide to get in instead of stemming it. The same chart (HW Dover) shows you an even more marked split of the east-going stream through the Straits themselves, part turning north and part running straight on along the Belgian coast.

Finding where the strongest and weakest tidal streams run is very much a matter of local knowledge; you can apply certain common-sense rules, but they do not always work. Let us consider first the case of finding the strongest favourable stream. The pattern of arrows and figures in the tidal atlas and the distance of the heaviest arrows (highest figures) from the shore will give you a good general idea of how far out to go (note that the tidal atlas charts have a latitude scale (up the sides) on which you can measure distance). Then look at the chart. First study the configuration of the bottom. Generally speaking, the tidal stream will run strongest down the middle of a constricted channel between, say, the shore and a bank or down the deep water just outside the outermost shallows, which is normally the main coastwise shipping lane. Sometimes the tide will run strongest along one channel in one direction and strongest along a different one in the other. The main stream will tend to move inshore and strengthen round a promontory and to maintain its line and weaken across a bay. Having formed a general picture, check it and fill out the details with the tables and marks on the chart. In this way you can arrive at an optimum course.

Conversely, if you have to stem a tide or cross a foul tide, it is normally best to stand right inshore or to head across banks and shallows *provided sea state and depth make it safe to do so*. The problem is that once you get into the wrong place you will be set back so much as you cross to try a new line that you are no better off. I have spent hours (normally five or six at a stretch!) of very hard work trying to find a way through a foul tide, sometimes in company with other boats. Generally speaking, one will not succeed without first-rate local knowledge. In most northern European waters it is probably wise to accept that small cruising yachts cannot round headlands with a foul wind and a foul tide; the only answer is to avoid this situation (see also Chapter 17).

Reverse currents, cross sets, tide rips, indications

We mentioned earlier in the chapter the inshore reverse current past Cherbourg; there are many examples of such effects, some widely known and used, some not. Basically you need local knowledge both to pick up such currents and to use them safely, even if they are described in books. Sometimes in calm water you can see the dividing line, generally known as a tide rip (Photo 13). The term 'tide rip' seems to be rather loosely used, sometimes synonymously with overfalls. However, as I have always understood it (and to my relief as

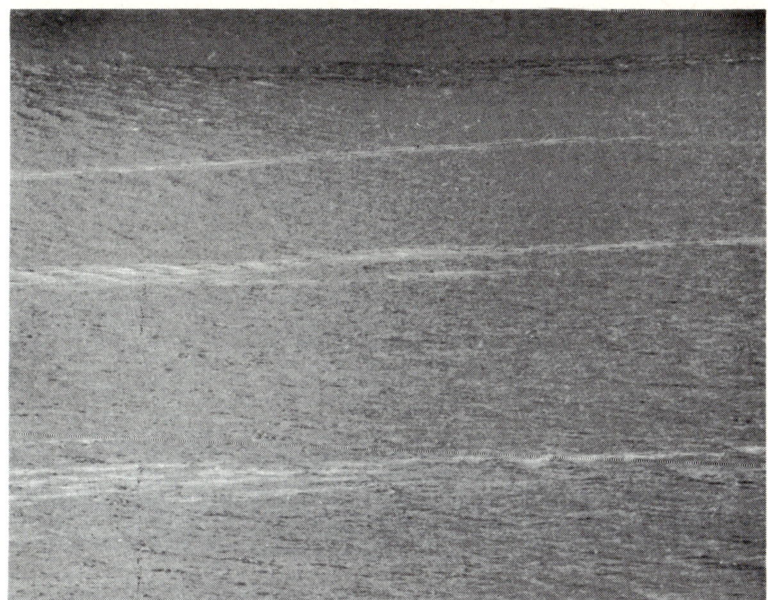

Photo 13. Tide rips. *This is in fact the head of Loch Inchard, with the discharge of the river running counter to the flood tide. The appearance however is completely characteristic of a tide rip pattern in calm water. (Author's photo.)*

Photo 14. *A closer view of one of the rips, showing the typical streaky, bubbly appearance.*

the *OED* defines it!), a tide rip is specifically a roughening of the water or at least a break in the surface pattern normally caused by the meeting of opposing currents. It is in fact the 'railway junction' I described the Hong Kong fishermen as using, and is not dangerous under most conditions provided you cross it deliberately or at least are aware of having done so. If you cross one inadvertently, and this is very easy to do at night or in fog, it can have exciting effects on your carefully planned navigation.

In estuaries, harbours and other confined waters, you have got to look at the shape of the shore-line and the actual state of the tide and envisage how the tide is going to flow. For instance, if you have a narrow channel between extensive sand or mud banks, there is going to be a moment on the flood at which the water reaches the lips of the banks and the tide starts to fill them (Figure 13). At this point, there is going to be a strong *cross current* or *cross set*, which will sweep you out of the channel and aground if you don't anticipate and watch for it.

In all confined and shallow waters, it thus becomes doubly important to make the best use of *indications of the strength and duration*

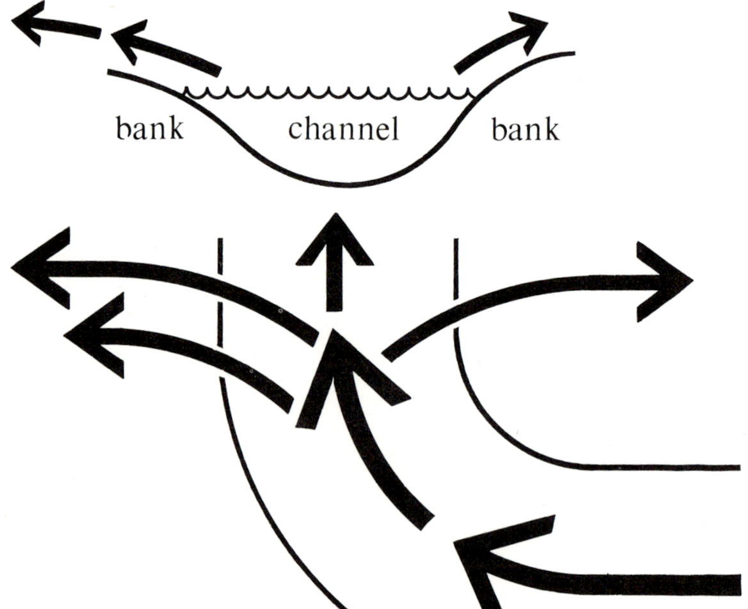

Figure 13. *Cross current caused by flooding of banks.*

of the tidal stream at the particular time and place you are in. We already mentioned the *set* of bouys (page 51). At sea the direction of the tidal stream is fairly predictable, and the main things a buoy can tell you about it are strength and maybe any abnormalities of duration. In sheltered waters and estuaries, however, the set of individual minor buoys – and of course the *lie of boats* on moorings and at anchor – give you a very good picture of the tidal conditions. I am going to venture some subjective yardsticks which will at least give you an idea of what to look for.

Approx. tidal stream	*Buoys*	*Craft anchored/on moorings*
0·5 k	Objects seen to move past; no set or wake	Most boats probably on wind-road or on former tide-road
1 k	Perceptible wake, no set	Mixed wind-road and tide-road (depending on wind force)
1·5 k	Wake 'ripply', slight set	
2 k	Wake marked, distinct set	All on tide-road
2·5 k	Wake 'bubbly', strong set	Taut chains/warps, easily visible wakes
3 k	Wake swirling, buoy starting to 'work'	Signs of pulling
3·5 k plus	Wake 'aggressive', buoy working	

Dangerous tide conditions – races, overfalls, eddies, etc.

Sometimes depth and configuration of bottom, high rates of flow, and/or a convergence of tidal streams create local conditions which are dangerous to yachts. They may cause loss of control, spin the boat causing an accidental gybe, or even stress the hull beyond its limits. Loss of control aggravated by damage in a strong tidal stream will almost certainly put the boat in serious difficulties and probably endanger life.

The largest in scale and most predictable of these effects is known as a *race*, the Portland Race for instance. A race will affect sea state and tidal streams over a wide area (Photo 15), much of which will be dangerous under almost all conditions. With a Force 5 or stronger wind against the tide it will produce a large danger zone. Races are very fully described in sailing directions and their local effects are

Photo 15. A typical race. *Note the area of broken water; the marginal conditions shown by the ripple pattern in front and to the right of the broken area; the arrow-shaped 'head' to the left (other races produce a 'tail', i.e. an extension* up-*tide of the main race). This is the Eynhallow Sound between Mainland and Rousay (Orkneys), further narrowed by the small island of Eynhallow in between.* (*Author's photo.*)

marked on medium- and large-scale charts. In making a coastwise passage you should give the races formed off headlands a very wide berth. When you have to pass through a race, as one does the Alderney Race, you must get the timing right, pick a precise line and hold strictly to it. There are in fact at least three lines through the Alderney Race which are safe in most conditions, even at springs, provided the wind is over the tide.

Local effects occurring in races, off promontories, on the edges of channels through bars or banks, and at other points when conditions change violently are marked on charts and described in 5011 Section O. *Overfalls* (Photo 16) are breaking waves caused by a strong tidal stream crossing rapidly shoaling water, an irregular bottom or underwater obstructions. The water almost literally 'falls over itself'. They are not always dangerous but are best avoided. *Breakers* are always a sign of danger; they can often be the first warning that one is heading into danger at night or in bad visibility. It is important to recognize broken water, which tends to be steep, short and irregular, as well as the more familiar, longer and more regular waves breaking on a bank that is nearly awash or a beach. *Eddies* (Photos 17 and 18) need no explanation. They are produced by water trying to get into or out of complex-shaped confined spaces. They are most likely to be

Photo 16. Characteristic overfalls *(in the same race as Photo 15). These cause very strong localized currents and eddies, which can spin a boat and gybe it or sweep it out of control. Note also the rather darker and steeper ripples (left and centre foreground) indicating marginal conditions.*

Photo 17. Overfalls round the edge of an eddy, *on the Horse Sand (mouth of River Deben). The channel is between the buoy and the far bank. The tide is flooding over the edge of the sand towards the camera, giving a cross-set effect (see Figure 13 and p. 80). (Author's photo.)*

Photo 18. An eddy, *on the edge of the River Deben bar (Woodbridge Haven, Suffolk). These will spin a slow-moving boat so that her way takes her onto the shingle before control is regained. Quick action with the engine will restore control. (Author's photo.)*

encountered and most dangerous at the edges of narrow channels through bars; they are apt to pluck one end of the boat and turn it straight on to the bar.

The concept and techniques of working the tide

In this chapter I have tried to explain the concept of *working the tide* and how to set about doing so. Knowing how many yachtsmen get into difficulties or at least meet with great frustration because they ignore tidal streams or do not research them with sufficient care, I have little hesitation in saying that working the tidal streams is the most important single message in this book.

There is no real substitute for first-hand local knowledge, but advice from harbour-masters or fishermen, good documentation and diligent research will go a long way towards getting the best out of the tides. Before a cruise involving passages of more than one tide, I make up my tidal atlas(es) as follows, putting a table on each of the thirteen charts: six-figure date–time group, time zone letter; estimated correction factor for neaps rate.

Suppose afternoon HW Dover on 11 May 1977 is 1757 Z = 1857 A, the range 4 m. Then my first entry on the table on the '6 hours before' chart will be:

111257 A – 1·25

I follow this through for each hour to the end of that tide and then start again for the next, the correction factor remaining constant throughout each tide, in fact throughout each day. You will find there is space to do this for three or four days (seven or eight entries at a time). I make the entries in soft pencil and strike them through or rub them out once they have passed, so that the top entry is the working one. I have then done in advance all the tricky bits where one can easily make a mistake – and got someone else to double check them! To find the tidal stream at any given place and time I have only to leaf through to the time in question, look at the nearest neaps figure to my position and apply the correction factor. (One can equally well work from springs figures with a correction factor of less than unity.) To get the correction factor:

1. Look up range in metres (on *Reed's* loose HW Dover card).
2. Convert to feet (pocket calculator or *Reed's* Section XVII).
3. Take any pair of tidal stream figures in waters where you expect to be during that tide.
4. Use graphical method recommended in tidal atlas (inside front cover).
5. Divide results by neaps figure. This gives factor.
6. Round factor to a figure you can use in your head.

Thus, in the example quoted:

Range Dover 11 May = 4 m = 13·1 ft.

(Off North Foreland at HW Dover) 13·24.

Lay off on graph between 13 and 24, 13·1 ft intercept gives 16 (i.e. 1·6 k).

16 ÷ 13 = 1·23 (pocket calculator), round to 1·25 which is: 'multiply by five, divide by four'.

Having done this, I am in a position to sum the tidal stream effects for a complete tide (6 hours) or a complete passage. I use the figure nearest to my expected position at the time, indicate a favourable stream with a '+' and an adverse stream with a '–', slack water being 0. Thus:

$$-04 + 25 + 15 + 11 + 06 + 0 = 53 = 5{\cdot}3 \text{ nm.}$$

I have then got the tidal stream information I need to start passage planning proper (Chapters 16 and 20). These later chapters will also explain how to allow for crossing tidal streams.

7
Errors

A sound philosophy of errors is among the most important pieces of the navigator's mental equipment. Unfortunately the conventional teaching and documentation of navigation – and indeed the rather taut and despotic attitude of some traditionally minded yachtsmen – militate against this. To steer clear of statistical theories we can perhaps borrow a pair of terms from the gunnery world and distinguish between 'mistakes' and 'errors'. *Mistakes* in this sense are instances of gross, avoidable human error – such as looking up a tide under the wrong month, mixing feet and metres or correcting a time or bearing in the wrong direction. Their magnitude is unpredictable but likely to be large, and their consequences are likely to be serious if not disastrous. Mistakes are unacceptable; this is why one always double checks data from two or more sources and whenever possible gets a second person to check calculations and plots.

Errors by contrast are something we must and indeed can learn to live with. The fact that plotting a three-bearing fix (Chapter 12) produces a 'cocked hat' or triangle of error and not a point intersection (Figure 14) is not the navigator's fault. Some people produce smaller cocked hats than others, but a clean three-line intersection is

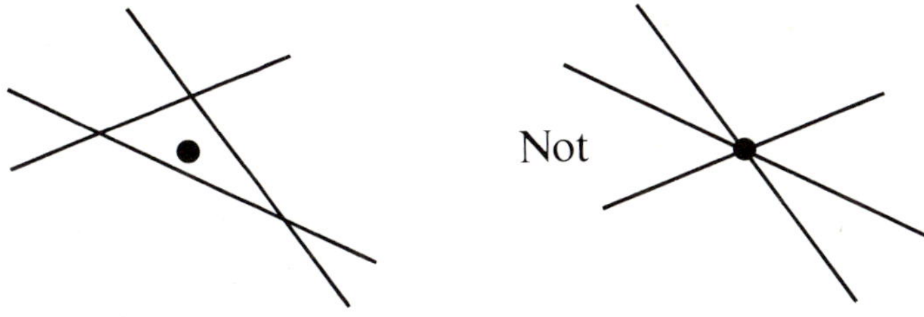

Figure 14. *Triangle of error.*

a fluke. After all, obtaining a guaranteed precise position of launch was said to be the greatest single problem in the development of submarine-launched ballistic missiles. If we look at the various types of error involved in navigating a typically equipped small yacht, we should be able to arrive at a sensible viewpoint.

Data errors

To start with, as you will already have appreciated, not all the splendid data on the acquisition of which I have laid such emphasis are quite what they seem. Information on marks is factual provided it is up to date: a buoy is a buoy and is pretty unlikely to have been swept out of position; the character and period of lights does not vary, though they may occasionally fail; and water-towers remain in one spot unless or until they are demolished. On the other hand, if *Reed's* said high water at Southwold entrance was at 1751 and you were watching a piece of wood drift in at 1750, you would be rather unlikely to see it start drifting out again at 1752. (In fact extremely unlikely, as the inflow at Southwold continues for around one hour after high water – but that is another story.) We have seen (Chapter 5) that weather conditions can affect tide heights and the duration of tidal streams by as much as 40–50 per cent and tidal stream rates by up to 100 per cent. We know the channel is shifting all the time on bars and the edges of some banks; but other soundings too may be slightly out.

I say this not to shake your confidence in the data but to emphasize that, although you have assembled the best possible data compiled and presented by first-class human and computer resources, this vast expertise is offering you predictions or expectancies rather than incontrovertible assertions. If you realize this, you can allow for variations in your planning and check the actual situation during your passage. If you accept every jot and tittle with blind faith, you may well come unstuck.

Instrument errors

In Chapter 2 I recommended simple but high quality instruments, but mentioned straight away that logs tended to read low at low speeds. Even if the instrument itself is accurate, it is difficult to design instruments that are free of *parallax* (Figure 15) when read from a distance.

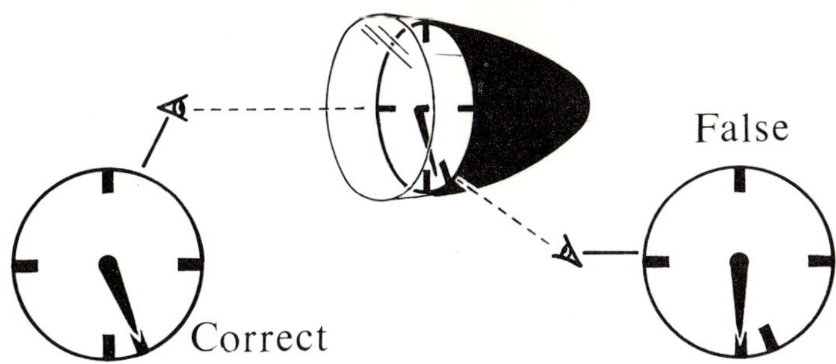

Figure 15. *Parallax error of reading instrument from an angle.*

Parallax affects compasses too, but they have a set of errors all of their own (see page 32). Compasses need to be heavily damped to be sensitive and easy to read; this means that the needle or card will swing off and back very slowly, as the boat yaws for instance, and a quick glance can lead to *needle swing* error. To overcome this you should *repeat every compass reading three times* ('take three cuts', as they say) before confirming it. Again, we have already seen that *magnetic variation* changes with time and place (see page 47). This 'second order variation' or change of variation is not normally one which the yacht navigator need take much account, but it is yet another source of error.

More serious is the problem of *compass deviation*, which may approach values as high as 10°. This can really matter if you take a series of bearings on a single object (running fixes, Chapter 12) with the hand-bearing compass, some just over the engine and others from the fore-deck. For your steering compass you can prepare a *deviation card*, and *Reed's* (Section VI) gives a very clear explanation of how to do this (see also page 32). But in my experience good modern compasses mounted well away from iron or steel masses and pre-calibrated with built-in correctors have very little deviation.

In fact, while emphasizing that a deviation card will often be required for binnacle-mounted compasses, especially in boats with a centre cockpit, I should like to use deviation as an example of using a sledge-hammer to crack a nut and smashing the dinner service instead. Suppose your steering compass in its working position actually has a deviation of 2–3° on its worst heading. I maintain that under the conditions in a small yacht there is going to be an error of up to ±1° (at least!) in observing a transit or recording a bearing on the instrument known as a *pelorus* (used to take bearings relative to the ship's head). A home-made pelorus is subject to plotting errors (see below) which I would estimate at ±2°. And there is an error of at least 1° (I believe considerably more) in reading a steering compass in its working position. *So this operation may produce an error between zero (if everything cancels out) and 4°, and since these are random errors you will have no idea which!* It is hardly sensible to use a method of this kind to detect and correct a suspected error of 3°. Admittedly, if you take eight or ten bearings to complete your deviation card, you will tend to smooth these errors out; but the validity of the smoothed deviation curve turns on a whole host of other assumptions.

Plotting errors

If you are sloppy about plotting, you are likely to get a cumulative plotting error large enough to have serious consequences. But under the conditions that prevail in a small yacht in a seaway, you are going to get errors however careful you are. A soft pencil line may be nearly 1 mm wide, and that is 1 km on a 1:1000000 chart. Depending on the shape of your pencil-point and the way you hold it, there may be a separation of up to 1 mm between the edge of the rule and the line; and this may vary from end to end, affecting the angle of the line by 30′ or so. Even with parallel rules correctly and carefully used, you may get an error of 1–2° in laying them on the compass rose (two error sources) and transferring the bearing; and protractors are in my experience liable to produce greater errors, not to mention mistakes from using the wrong effective centre. Similarly laying off distances may produce errors of up to 0·5 nm. if you have to interpolate between latitude marks on a smallish-scale chart. We shall explore techniques and problems of plotting in Chapter 10, but you will see that one must expect an error of, say, *1°30′ and/or 0·5 nm. in each operation*; and these individual errors may be cumulative over the plot as a whole.

System errors

So far we have considered the errors arising in individual instruments or procedures. Let us now consider two actual situations or 'systems'. The first is the helmsman steering a compass course without the aid of a suitable mark ahead.

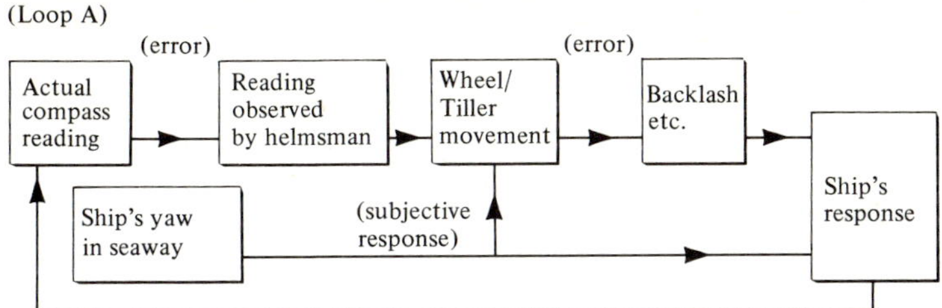

Without probing deeper into this, we can see two things. First, the accuracy with which the ordered heading is steered depends largely on how well the helmsman subconsciously averages the inputs of compass and ship's movement (subjective response); at any given moment the ship could be up to 5° or more off the ordered heading. Second, with the markings on a typical steering compass, the best the helmsman can hope to do is to hold on a 5° mark or between two 5° marks. If you order him to steer '234° M' he will wear himself out to little purpose. But if you say: 'Between 230 and 235 but a bit towards 235', you have set him a reasonable task.

In the second case we can consider navigation too:

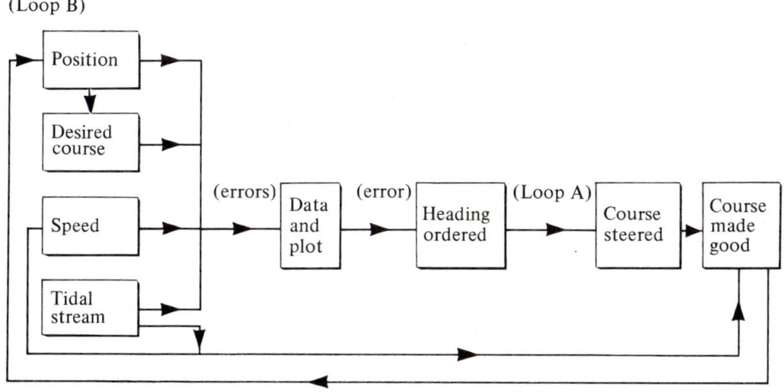

Here we have four inputs, three of them subject to primary errors and the fourth, desired course, subject to a secondary error arising from position error. We have already looked at the order of magnitude of plotting errors which may affect the heading ordered and at the 'steering a compass course' loop (Loop A). Variations of speed from the predicted value and of tidal stream rate from the book will come in again as sources of error in the course made good. And then you go back and start again from a new estimated position.

Comparison of navigational and data errors

Perhaps we can come at this another way by considering a medium-length passage, say the crossing from Poole to Cherbourg. The distance from Poole Bar buoy to Cherbourg outer mark is about 60 nm. With moderate visibility we might hope to get a visual fix of our position about 12 nm. out of Poole and some 10 nm. off the French coast. Let us say we have a leg of 40 nm. between these positions, and that we expect to sail this in eight to nine hours or one and a half tides. Now suppose we have a Force 5–6 Southwesterly following a gale, so that the flood stream is 30 per cent above predicted rate and 'overruns' for an hour, the ebb being correspondingly below par. This is going to put our landfall about 6 nm. east of where we expect. (From experience, a typical east–west error on this landfall is 3 nm.)

Now suppose, looking at the section above, that we make a net error of 3° in heading ordered and one of the two watches has a 2° bias in its course, we have a net error of $(3 + 2/2) = 4°$, or around 3 nm. over a distance of 40 nm. This is around half the error caused by tidal stream in our example and about the same as the typical landfall error on this passage. *Generally speaking, under the conditions prevailing in a small cruising yacht, the net navigational error is of the same order as the net error caused by variations between data and actual conditions.* The two may of course compound or cancel each other out; and you cannot know which.

Living with inaccuracy

The existence of these two groups of errors and the fact that they are similar in magnitude does not however mean that the navigator should not or cannot do anything about them. The navigator who makes his plan, gets it double checked, orders the heading from Poole Bar and turns in is apt to wake up, in our example, to find himself charging inexorably down the Alderney Race in the early morning mist with the rest of the crew gazing at him expectantly.

The good navigator will order a provisional heading and then spend an hour or so using his senses, his instruments and the seat of his pants to get a complete read of the actual situation and give an improved heading. Some of the techniques he can use are described later in this book; but what really matters is attitude of mind. Once he is satisfied he has got the boat pointing in the best direction, he will indeed turn in but with a request to be woken if conditions change, at the first sight of land or a light and in any event when there are fifty miles on the log. If he sees the Cherbourg landmarks dead on the nose, he will look smug and go below for breakfast; but he will know that this is something of a fluke. If not, he will not be surprised. He will probably know which way he has tended to bias his plan and work to find out where he is and order a correction in good time.

The first lesson is then to expect errors and to set vigorously about minimizing them as soon as information on actual conditions is acquired. The second is to allow for errors by *good safety margins in time and space*. By all means make an ideal plan; but make a pessimistic one too and operate at whatever point between the two is suggested by your feel for the magnitude and direction of probable errors.

When high accuracy matters

I am convinced that under most conditions relaxed acceptance of the possibility of errors combined with a very vigorous effort to keep on top of them and progressively improve the situation represents the most effective approach. There are however a number of circumstances which call for a flat-out effort to minimize errors at source. One obvious case is a long leg without any opportunity to check your position (other than by celestial navigation or DF radio). Another is in dangerous or confined waters – a Scylla and Charybdis situation where you cannot allow your normal margins against one danger without exposing yourself to another. But undoubtedly the most nerve-racking, difficult and genuinely dangerous one of all is fog; we shall be discussing this fully in Chapter 18.

8

Pilotage

Most passages within sight of land require excellent documentation but can be made *in good visibility* without resort to instruments other than binoculars and maybe a stop-watch for 'counting' lights (see page 65). They cannot be made *safely* without the instruments described in Chapter 2 and the skills needed to use them and described in the second part of this book, *because of the risk of visibility closing down.* As you move away from sheltered waters and buoyed channels, the use of navigational techniques will increasingly make your passage faster, more controlled and thus safer. But I want to deal in this chapter with *the visual techniques independent of instruments* generally known as *pilotage.* And I want to do this for two reasons: to bridge the gap from map-reading to basic navigation; and to put pilotage and navigation in perspective for the average cruising yachtsman.

An analogy may be helpful here. Suppose that you drive from London up the M1 for a weekend's walking on the Yorkshire Moors. You will need to *time* your departure from London and your crossing of the Leeds/Bradford conurbation to miss the respective rush hours. You will have looked up routes and decided to use the M1; once you reach the approaches to it you can work entirely off sign-posts. To get through the built-up area after you leave the motorway you will need to use the map, sign-posts, street names and maybe landmarks. Once you are out on the minor road of your choice, you will be working from the map with some help from sign-posts, but you will need to check constantly against landmarks and major features, and from the 'lie of the land'. On your walks you will be using the map, landmarks, major features and the lie of the land, together with the occasional cairn or fingerpost. And if the mist comes down you will be dependent on map and compass, with some help from the lie of the land in the shape of gradients.

This is all very like making your way down a river, out through a buoyed channel and along the coast to make another entrance and anchor in a quiet creek. The differences are: *tide is a much sterner master than rush-hour traffic*; and *there is no 'lie of the sea'*, or at least not much. What pilotage – and this chapter – are really about is creating for yourself, with the aid of documentation, navigation marks and landmarks, a visually identifiable 'lie of the sea'.

Inland/inshore passage planning

Once you have assembled the requisite documentation and made a first study of it, take a chart covering the whole passage (if possible) and, using dividers and the latitude scale up the side (see page 47), work out the approximate distance. It is a good rule to add 10 per cent, just as one does for road journeys. Knowledge of your boat and the weather forecast will then give you an approximate *passage time ignoring tide*.

Next look at the *tide problem*, using the data and techniques described in Chapter 6. Generally speaking, in an 'out–along–in' passage you will be going with or against the tidal stream, not across it. Study the *far end first*; decide from the chart, tidal information, and sailing directions whether you have to go in on the flood and whether you only have enough water to get in at certain times. Then look at the *exit problem*. Normally you make exits on the ebb, but dangerous ones may have to be made at high water or even on the flood; if the sailing directions say this, they mean it! All you need to establish at this stage is any *absolute limitations on leaving harbour or entering*; if these exist you may have to plug a tide or part of one after you clear harbour, or to anchor off and wait at the far end. Next look at the coastwise tidal stream, and work out *how many miles of tide you can get under you* (see page 85); this gives you your *net coastwise distance*. Then, in the same way, sum up what you will get out of or lose from the tide while clearing and entering harbour. Note here that there may be a difference of several hours between high or low water at the entrance and further inland. You will then be left with three sets of distances and times:

1. EXIT: restrictions, optimum timing.
2. COASTWISE LEG(S): optimum timing, duration.
3. ENTRANCE: restrictions, optimum timing.

If these tie in you have no problem. Otherwise you have a decision to make on where you are going to take the foul tide. You thus arrive at *a time to leave moorings*.

You will now know at what state of the tide you will be at any given place on your passage and will have found *depths above chart datum*, or at least will have determined whether these are critical, and if so, where. You can then use the charts, in particular the soundings, to *decide on your exact course*. You must give a very wide berth – even a mile or two – to *dangers that will be to leeward or downtide of you*, to *shoals lying to leeward of you* whatever the tide, and to *all shoals on an ebb tide*. On the other hand, provided you double check and allow a reasonable margin, you may reap a great dividend in time and effort from taking a short cut with an offshore breeze on a flood tide.

Having chosen your course, decide which marks, landmarks or features you are going to work on, and also those which you may see, or may need if you have to change your plan or to beat (Chapter 17). Make a *quick reference list* of these, *including light and* SOUND *characteristics*. Sound signals are often forgotten about when planning on a clear day but needed very badly and very quickly if you fail to spot a light in time or if fog suddenly comes down.

This planning procedure will provide you with a safe course and a realistically timed passage. What is more, in going through it you will have built up in your mind and your notes a pretty good picture of the area of land and sea you are interested in.

Let me clarify the main features of this procedure by the example of my own situation; you can then do the same exercise with your home data. The mouth of the River Bure in Yarmouth Haven (Norfolk) is narrow with two very low bridges and a very fast ebb that continues to run for two hours after low water at Yarmouth Bar. The mouth of the Bure is dangerously full of Norfolk Broads motor-cruisers, mostly hired to people who may be completely inexperienced; they use it to cross between the Bure and the southern rivers of the Broads. My only safe time to clear these bridges by day is low water slack; at night, when there is no hire-boat traffic, I can come down on the ebb an hour or two earlier. I then have to raise the mast and get ready for sea, so that I either have to clear Gorleston (Yarmouth Haven) entrance with between three and five hours of flood (southward) stream outside, or lie against the wall in Yarmouth mixing it with the oil-shipping and fishing traffic. If I am going south, this is fine; I catch the tide down to Southwold (about 15 nm.), where I can safely enter or leave between two hours after low water and two hours after high (a good indication, this, of the difference in acceptable risk between flood and ebb), and sit out an ebb in comfort to get over the trauma of Yarmouth Haven. Although some of the entrances round the Suffolk coast are very limited as to safe entry and exit times, one can in fact 'tide-hop' the lot. Going home I catch the ebb from Southwold, and the first flood up the Bure, but timing things to get round Orford Ness and into Southwold is another story. If I am headed north from Gorleston, I normally in fact clear harbour and plug the rest of the flood stream, so that I am well poised to make use of the following ebb.

Use of binoculars

Rather few people know how to use binoculars properly, and thus either see far less than they might or – I sometimes suspect – unintentionally copy the Nelson touch. Always hang binos round your neck having adjusted their strap so that you can bring them straight up to your eyes and they will not swing wide as you move about. Keep them clean with optical tissue or clean, dry Kleenex-type tissue and always clean them off after exposure to moisture or sea water.

The first thing is to establish your *inter-ocular distance* (IOD). This will be a figure between 64 and 72 mm for a grown man. Your oculist can tell it you; it is in fact the setting at which the eyepieces fit comfortably and closely to both your eyes. You set the binos to it by means of a scale. Your binos may have separate focussing – i.e. a scale on each eyepiece. These scales go either side of 0; for interest, they are in units known as 'diopters'. Close your weaker eye and focus for your better one; then close that and focus for the weaker one. Finally you may need to make a slight balancing adjustment with both eyes open. When you get the binos properly set, the image will suddenly blend and acquire clarity and depth.

Modern binoculars usually have centre-wheel focussing with an individual adjustment on one eyepiece only. First focus on the centre-wheel for the eye without the separate adjustment. Then close the eye without the separate adjustment and focus the individual eyepiece. It takes several attempts to get this right. It is worth making a note of your bino settings, particularly if several people are using the same pair in turn.

Depth, wave pattern and water colour

We discussed various tide conditions on pages 78–84. In daylight you can do a good deal to make sure you are safe and on course by observing the sea. Deep water looks dark and grey, blue or green; shallow water looks lighter-coloured and brownish or yellowish – muddy or sandy. If you are inshore of the main shelf with say 4–5 m under you, you will often be able to see the limits of the deep water offshore of you and of the marginal but safe water you have chosen on the inshore side. You can thus, other things being equal, position yourself by the colour band – as of course you can do on the edge of the deep water channel.

If there is a sea running, the waves from deep water may be very large and violent but will tend to be long and regular with the occasional 'big one'. The wave pattern over shallow water will be shorter, steeper and irregular – often 'messy-looking' in fact. Then of course there comes the point of incipient breakers. An experienced *ear* can distinguish relative depths in rather the same way by night or in bad visibility from the characteristic sound of the waves.

It is extremely difficult to explain or illustrate these points in a book. But if you are aware of them – and of their importance for safety – study of the sea and of soundings on the chart will give you an eye and finally an ear for them.

Transits on landmarks and navigation marks

The transit is one of the key techniques of pilotage; there are four basic cases of it (Figure 16; see also page 62). Case 1 is that of homing in on two leading marks or lights; a straight line of the three points – the two marks and your boat – establishes a unique *position line*. Case 2 is the converse of this and normally applies when leaving harbour. Frequently (Case 3) it will be necessary to hold a transit between a buoy astern, say a bar buoy or a safe-water mark, and a single mark ahead; this is a most important safety procedure which needs a certain amount of practice. Marks on land may of course be beacons, or buildings such as water-towers or church spires, or natural features such as peaks or nicks in cliff-lines, or a mixture of these.

A beam transit (which need not be exactly abeam) can be taken between two objects on land, or a buoy and a landmark or two buoys.

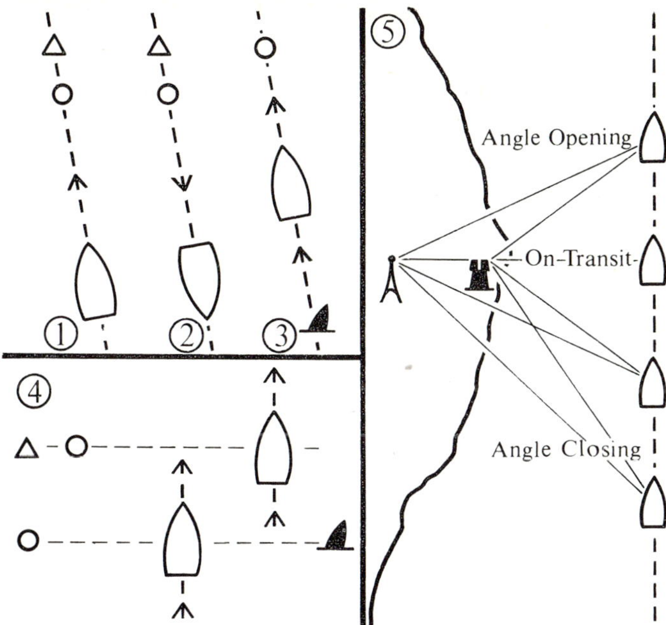

Figure 16. *Basic types of transit.*

It can in fact be done with the boat between the two marks, but this, like Case 3, is rather more difficult. The important thing is that the distance between the two objects on the line of sight should be sufficient; this depends on your distance from the nearer object and other factors such as how well the objects stand out. There must be no risk of confusing the two objects or of their being so close to one another or to you that a change in your position will not be immediately apparent.

The commonest use of a beam transit is to find out whether or not you are 'making' past the land, for instance when beating and/or against a foul tide. For this purpose the objects need not be in line – in fact they will not be. What you are looking for is a closing of the angle until you are on transit, and then an opening of it. Marks on the beam in transit, that is marks which you see as in line, give you a position line. In combination with a nearby mark or a fore-and-aft transit this will fix your position. Alternatively it may tell you when you have reached the point at which to change course or tack. Transits are a most useful aid; you should try to pick them off the chart when preparing the passage, and identify and make use of any that appear as you are under way.

Logging position

If you are outside harbour or at least outside truly sheltered waters, you may need at any time to switch from the simple visual techniques of pilotage to navigation proper. The same thing happens of course as you stand out to sea, but then you are expecting it. We shall see that to use navigational techniques you must start with a known datum position. If you are in a buoyed channel, you may be able to fix your position without further ado or simply by closing a mark and starting from there.

Basically however you need to know where you are at any given moment, and this can be quite difficult. Unless you take bearings or use a transit, you may be seriously out as to how far along the coast with respect to a key landmark you in fact are; experience suggests that an error of judgement equal to your distance off the coast is quite possible here. In other words your working definition of 'on the beam' may suddenly become optimistic by as much as 45° even if your heading is parallel to the coast. If you are beating, and this is when optimism is most liable to set in, it is very easy to forget that your beam may be laid at any angle up to 80° off the line of the coast when you are on the seaward tack. Oddly enough I have never known anyone make this mistake over a beam fix while on an inshore tack and arrive at a pessimistic estimate of position – optimism is the navigator's worst enemy! Likewise visual estimation of your distance off the coast, like all visual range-finding, is subject to unbelievably high errors – again usually on the optimistic side.

A conscious effort is therefore required to know your position. Whenever you know it precisely you should record it in the deck-log (see page 114), together with other key information of the moment. Remember particularly to check your position and log it when you tack; otherwise if you have to go over to navigational techniques you will be completely lost. If you have a log streamed/switched on, you should also record the reading of this to establish a datum.

Allowances for tide

We have assumed that when using pilotage you will be generally headed with or against the tide or tidal stream, but this is not always entirely true. You may in fact sail across it when clearing a bar or, much more important, entering harbour – or of course if you have to beat in or out. There is a cross (coastwise) set across many entrances formed by open-work jetties; this is usually indicated in the sailing directions but should always be expected. There is also of course a cross set in the early and middle stages of a long entrance, when you are in fact still in the coastwise tidal stream; entering St Malo on the flood is a particularly good example of this in terms both of the strength of set and the danger of ignoring it.

If you are using navigational techniques proper, your heading will have allowed for this set. But in pilotage you must judge how to counteract it. Great care is needed to stay within the channel, although you may be headed for a mark. Keeping on transit, or if necessary just off it, between one channel marker and the next, is a particularly useful aid, and you should also pick longer-range transits to check on. A strong cross set, however, like reduced visibility, is one of the situations which brings you out of the realm of simple pilotage into that of using some of the navigational techniques which form the subject of the chapters that follow.

9

Landfalls

In the previous chapter we looked at the techniques used in moving through sheltered waters and marked channels, and noted how the need for navigational techniques as such increased as we moved from sheltered waters to open coastal waters and/or out to sea. To get this problem of navigational techniques in perspective, we should perhaps look next at the transition back from navigation to pilotage – the making of a landfall, or more precisely the identification of it. Very few yachtsmen – I hope none who are not well beyond profiting from this book – will make passages long enough for the mere sight of land to become an occasion for near-hysterical rejoicing. What matters to us is which bit of land it is. On the other hand we must all admit to ourselves that the sight of land or the loom of a light located on land produces a disproportionate psychological response; and that, however good the conditions, we all have a deep-seated desire to see these. Early morning light or reduced visibility can all too easily turn a cloud into a headland, complete with all its identifying features, or amplify the noise of the sea to sound like shoaling. Pie-in-the-sky landfalls are the most severe individual cases of the optimism which besets most navigators – and indeed yachts' crews in general.

Once again you will probably get the best out of this chapter by considering a piece of coast you know well with a port in its centre and a strong tidal stream. In writing this, I have approaching the Cotentin Peninsula to enter Cherbourg (Admiralty Chart No. 1106) particularly in mind.

Advance estimation of error

In closing the Cotentin Peninsula from the North you do well to aim pretty well at the middle, because otherwise there is a significant risk in bad conditions of missing the end altogether and finishing up down the Alderney Race or in the Seine Bay. When this risk does not arise it is best to aim for the port until you are near enough to be certain which direction the tidal stream will be flowing when you close the coast, and then to adjust your heading slightly to make sure that, within the normal error zone, you *close the coast up-tide of your objective*. Getting down-tide of it can easily cost you six hours if you can enter at any state of the tide and twelve if you cannot. Tidal streams apart, it is much better to be reasonably sure which side of the port you are in case visibility is poor when you close. On the other hand, don't aim off so much that you need a new passage plan to get into harbour.

Tidal stream is a major factor in estimating your probable landfall, and its effects can be rather unpredictable. For example I recall heading for Poole from Cap de la Hague, coming up south-west of the Needles and getting caught in the tail end of the Portland Race springs ebb with a Force 7–8 wind over it. There was no danger, in fact it was a super sail; but a series of fixes showed us to be making towards Poole Bar in a zigzag without ever changing our heading.

Clearly wind and visibility will be other factors in your choice of approach, or you may steer to pick up a particular mark or make a landfall on a conspicuous feature. All in all, it is rather seldom a question of just pointing the boat at your objective and hoping you will hit it on the nose.

Identifying features

If you are to stand any chance of identifying a landfall quickly in poor light or under difficult conditions, you must make yourself fully familiar in advance with all the information you have about the coast. Both official and unofficial sailing directions may help you in this, both by describing how features or stretches of coast will first appear from particular angles of approach, and by highlighting confusing or deceptive features. What is more you must list the references of this information and particularly of any diagrams or photographs. You need to do your homework very thoroughly indeed if you are not to be caught out. To repeat an example mentioned earlier, anyone seeing the Barfleur and Cap de la Hague lighthouses on a clear day with the ground visible behind them would say it was impossible to mix them up. Likewise at night the characters of their lights are quite distinct. But try half-light on a misty morning with an onshore wind and a flood stream, so that you cannot stand in too close. With the mist shutting out all the background, you have only the heights and visual characteristics of the two towers to go by. How often does one study these when one looks up a light? In my case at least, once too seldom.

By *confusing features* one may mean a single feature which looks very different from different angles – such as in fact the Cap de la Hague lighthouse, which appears to stand on the end of a long spit (or an isolated rock) viewed from the north-east and to be on a hump nestling under the cliff when seen from the north-west. Alternatively two similar features such as two spires or a water-tower and a silo may be confused with one another when you can see only one of them.

Deceptive features are perhaps best exemplified by channels which make a right-angled turn just inside the entrance, so that the far bank appears to be a continuation of the main shoreline if you close them square. Three examples of this problem of 'finding the hole' are the Cherbourg main entrance (concrete fortifications), Gorleston (open-work jetties, also difficult at night because of shore lights) and the River Ore in Suffolk (shingle banks).

You also need to study the relevant medium- and large-scale charts with great care, particularly of course any shore profiles or notes/observations (Chapter 4). It is not easy to visualize from a plan what you will see in elevation as you close; it may be worth trying to sketch a profile for yourself – and it will certainly be interesting to compare this with the reality! This is incidentally a good way to train oneself in studying charts carefully and making use of *all* the detail they show. Remember in particular that *you will not see all the ground when you first sight land.* To reinforce this look at Table I – Distance of Sea Horizon in Nautical Miles in Section VII of *Reed's* and at the diagram on the preceding page. To drive this point home with a second example, it means that when directly closing a shore in good visibility you may first see the top of a 50 m yellow sandstone cliff as a beach. The most striking example I know of this is the south-west aspect of the Isle of Wight already mentioned (see page 49 and profile on Admiralty Chart No. 2045).

The problem of firmly identifying a landfall and, from it, your exact position, is a difficult and sometimes contentious problem (see pages 122–30 for a further discussion).

Correcting action, course for entrance

Let us suppose that when you identify the landfall and your position you are 2 nm. up-tide of your desired course and 8 nm. out, and you can see the entrance or a feature locating it. The most common mistake at this stage is to heave a sigh of relief and turn straight for the entrance, finishing up hopelessly and helplessly down-tide of it. You will have been steering a heading that allows for tide (Chapter 16), and the fact that you can now see land makes no difference whatever to what wind and tide will do to you.

Far from switching off with the aid of coffee and bacon and eggs, or a large whisky, you now have to sit down and make a mini passage plan all over again. You have got to work out (Chapter 16 again) what heading to steer to go in *a straight line from your position to the entrance or some chosen point off it*. Remember here that both navigator and helmsman must be aware that the tide is setting you along the coast and *no one landmark can be used to steer on for more than a few minutes* (see also Chapter 11). If there is any risk of fog you must set up the DF radio (Chapter 13) and, more obviously, if you are not going to get in in daylight you must recheck all lights you may need.

If you are going to approach the entrance at an angle to the normal channel, you have got to check that you will have enough water under you, and more particularly that you will be able to *pick up and turn on to leading marks or lights in time*. For a small yacht this second factor is far more likely to be the limiting one. It is dangerous to come suddenly round the corner into the channel with no time to orientate yourself and the helmsman, and neither time nor space to take avoiding action if a ship is coming out. In easy entrances to major ports, there is no reason why you should not take reasonable short cuts, provided you allow yourself time and space to come at the entrance itself in the right direction.

In closing major ports with difficult entrances, minor ports or estuaries, you will need to be a good deal more careful. We shall be exploring this further in Chapter 19, but one might say there are two ground rules in such cases:

1. Find, identify and close the outer mark before committing yourself to making the entrance.
2. Even if you are on leading marks or lights, locate and identify each successive channel or danger marker, holding offshore of it until you have done so.

St Malo is a very good example of the need for extreme care, the more so as there is a strong tide set *across* the trickiest part of the channel with some particularly sharp rocks just on either side of it.

Night landfalls

Under northern European conditions, it is usually much easier to close and enter well-lit major ports, even those with difficult entrances, by night than by day. To start with you will see only the major lights; these are easily identifiable and allow you to fix your position as often as you want with minimal risk of confusion. Light buoys can (usually) be seen further off by night, and are certainly more easily identifiable at a distance by their light character than by their physical characteristics. The only likely problems are shore lights and poor visibility (psychologically at least always more difficult to deal with at night).

Minor ports and estuaries, on the other hand, and unlit or poorly lit coasts in general, should be approached only by day and in good visibility, unless you are thoroughly familiar with them and you know your position precisely and reliably from the use of navigational techniques. It is here above all that 'the best aid to navigation is to have been there before'.

Finally a point of seamanship, but one that also affects the navigator vitally in the true sense of that word. However tired you all may be, however hairy the conditions at sea and however brightly the neon lights on the waterfront joints twinkle, there is only one safety rule by night or day: 'If in doubt, stand out.'

10

Plotting and Logging

So far, I think, I have involved the reader in nothing worse than the four basic operations of arithmetic. These are unfortunately necessary to deal with tidal effects in waters one does not know but can be done without difficulty on a pocket calculator. By contrast I have tried to impress on you the need for great persistence in acquiring information and for diligence in using it. And I hope the last two chapters will have defined the points at which the yachtsman must resort to position-finding techniques other than simple observation, first as an aid to his eyes and then, once he loses sight of land, as an essential technique for getting where he wants. Nonetheless I believe that most cruising yachtsmen will do well to regard navigation as an art rather than a numerical science, to educate the seat of their pants by reading, observation and experience rather than to take an evening class in mathematics.

Use of plotting instruments

The use of plotting instruments is really very simple. The desperate struggle some people have with this in attempting to learn navigation from orthodox teaching stems maybe from a kind of Howard Bateman situation – the instructor cannot conceive that any student does not know, or cannot immediately see, what to do; and the students dare not tell him how wrong he is.

Protractors

Let us start with an instrument which I personally do not use – the protractor. I can see no reason why anyone who uses Admiralty

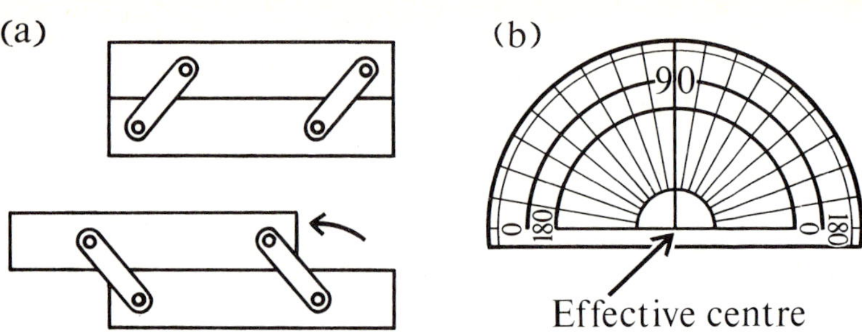

Figure 17(a) *Parallel rules, closed and extended positions.* (b) *Effective centre of a protractor.*

charts and has a flat surface to put them on should do so. There are numerous patent protractors, some with swing arms, which are claimed to, and probably do, perform magic feats for you; there are circular protractors which look rather impressive. But if you feel that for you the way to measure or lay off angles is a protractor, then start with a schoolboy's semicircular one. The whole problem about protractors is first identifying the effective centre and second remembering to use this as opposed to the mid-point of the base or whatever. Figure 17*b* shows the centre of a schoolboy protractor; if you use something more complicated you must be absolutely clear where the centre lies and how it is marked.

Parallel rules

The compass rose on a chart gives you a means of laying off and measuring angles by using *parallel rules* (see page 42). I prefer the 'walking' (Captain Field's) to the rolling kind, because it is very difficult, especially in a seaway, to know whether the rolling kind have slipped between rose and plot; also you cannot move them endways. With the walking kind, one always knows if they have slipped (if one is prepared to admit it to oneself!) and with a certain amount of cunning one can transfer the angle with equal ease in any required direction. Take a set of rules (Figure 17*a*) and note first that when their inner edges are together the links will point obliquely in one direction when the ends are also together and in the other when the rules are, so to speak, extended to full length. Note also that the width of the rules is substantial in relation to all but the largest-scale charts. Like most right answers in navigation, the easy and accurate use of parallel rules is largely a matter of planning – in this case planning how to minimize the distance you have to move the rules and the number of 'steps'.

First lay the rules *between* the rose and the position you are interested in and with their long edges roughly on the bearing you want. Then work out which way to swing them to get any endways displacement you want, and pre-set them accordingly. Then lay the nearer outer edge:

along the position line if you want to measure its bearing, *or*
on the rose (see below) if you want to draw a line through a point on a given bearing.

Then walk the rules in the way you have planned to bring any one of the four parallel edges on to the rose or on to the point you are interested in. When drawing a line, make sure the pencil is angled away from the edge so that the point runs hard against the edge; this is in fact a common and significant source of error.

A second common source of error is the setting of the rules on the rose, whether one is going from or to it. *The working edge of the rule must pass through the centre of the rose* (Figure 18); a quite small error here will produce a significant difference in bearing. Being clumsy I normally check this by also reading off the *back-bearing*, i.e. the opposite direction, and checking that bearing and back-bearing differ by 180°. Double check too that you are using the part of the rose you want – normally the magnetic ring.

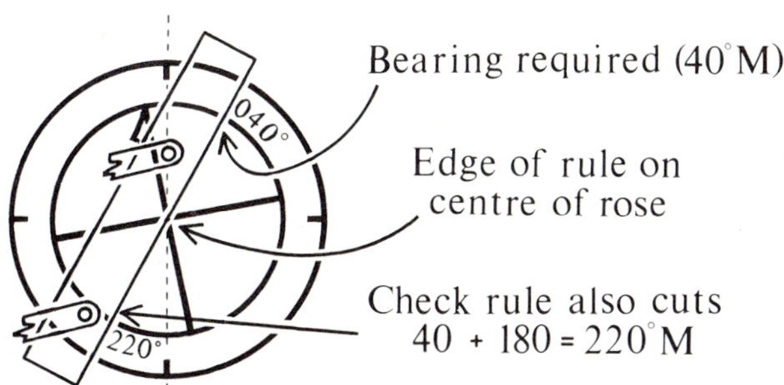

Figure 18. *Laying off a bearing.*

Dividers

On page 42 I recommended 'single-handed' dividers. You hold these between your thumb and the first two fingers, so that you can adjust them by a kind of rolling action. When using dividers you will nearly always be working between a position line or two marks and the latitude scale. Choose a convenient point on the scale as your 'zero'; this should normally be a unit degree, e.g. 55°00′. Ring it in soft pencil on both sides of the chart. On large-scale charts you may sometimes have to use a 10′ mark as zero, but you will probably be measuring distances less than 10 nm. so there is no problem.

When using dividers, *don't* press them right into the paper to make visible holes; this will both ruin the chart and lead to inaccuracies. Put one leg on to your zero or base mark first, just firmly enough to hold. Then adjust the other. Then check that the first has not moved. You will then read off or lay off the correct distance; if laying it off on a position line, mark the point lightly in pencil before removing the dividers.

Compasses

I have never understood why the use of a pair of compasses is regarded as a heresy. Admittedly one can strike an invisible arc with dividers, but why not do things the easy way? To use compasses easily and accurately, cut a hard pencil to a suitable short length and keep it sharp. Don't press hard. You may need two sizes of compass, as you will get handling problems and inaccuracy if you set them to too wide an angle; 60° between the legs is about the limit if you are to avoid the risk of the pencil point sliding outwards as you turn the compasses.

Basic plotting techniques

To make a simple navigational diagram, known as a plot, on the chart, you need two pairs of basic techniques and one single procedure.

Angles

Use the *parallel rules* and the *compass rose* to measure a line through a point on a given bearing. *Normally you can work entirely off magnetic bearings*, but use the rose and the rules (or any straight edge) to convert between true and magnetic.

Distances

Use the *dividers* and the *latitude scale* (up the sides of the chart) to measure the distance in nautical miles between two points, or to lay off a distance from a given point on a line already drawn.

Arcs and radii

Use the *compasses*, setting them on the latitude scale, to draw a circle of given radius about a point or to *strike an arc* (Figure 19). You do this either to find the point of intersection of two circles or (more usually) to find a point C on a line AC at a given distance from another point B.

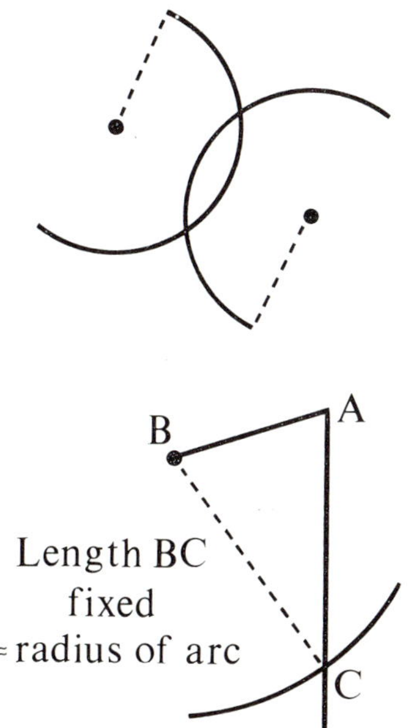

Figure 19. *Striking an arc (two examples).*

As you gain experience, you will find it is seldom necessary to draw complete lines or circles. Just put in the bit or bits you need. Unnecessary markings on a chart will shorten its life and may obliterate an important symbol.

Abbreviated notations

One of the purposes of this book is to steer the reader clear of formal definitions and protocol, but it is important in long passages (and of course in ocean racing) that one watch should be able to understand the other's notes. I am therefore going to list symbols and abbreviations I myself use (apart from those I use only for taking down weather forecasts).

Times and dates

Always use the twenty-four-hour clock and write the time as a four-figure group, e.g. 1234. As we saw, however, in Chapters 5 and 6, you need to be absolutely clear what time you are talking about. Most tables are based on Greenwich Mean Time (GMT) otherwise known as Z or ZULU time. A time one hour ahead of GMT is A or ALPHA time, two hours ahead B or BRAVO, and so on. Thus 1200 Z=1300 A=1400 B. . . . The full list reads:

Hours ahead *of GMT*	*Zone suffix*	*Hours* behind *GMT*	*Zone suffix*
1	A	1	N
2	B	2	O
3	C	3	P
4	D	4	Q
5	E	5	R
6	F	6	S
7	G	7	T
8	H	8	U
9	I	9	V
10	K	10	W
11	L	11	X
12	M	12	Y

GMT: Z

Thus to define the time completely, and particularly to avoid wrong use of tide tables, you must identify the time with a letter, e.g. 1234 A.

I am not going into the problems of the International Date Line, but for marking charts, logging and tabulating (see pages 84–86), you need to identify date as well as time. This gives a group of six figures and one letter, e.g. 012345 B or 210123 Z, known as a *date-time group*.

Annotation of charts

Apart from the date-time group, I use two symbols, each of them in two forms:

× for an uncorrected position, normally dead reckoning (Chapter 14).
△ for a position relating to a fix (Chapter 12).
⊙ for any other corrected position.

I use *full lines and a solid dot for positions achieved and confirmed, and broken lines and a ring for expected positions*:

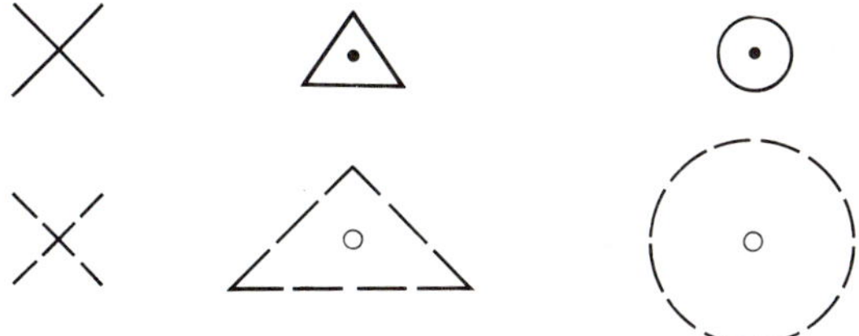

In fact for the last one (broken circle) I try to shape and scale it to indicate the error zone I expect, e.g.

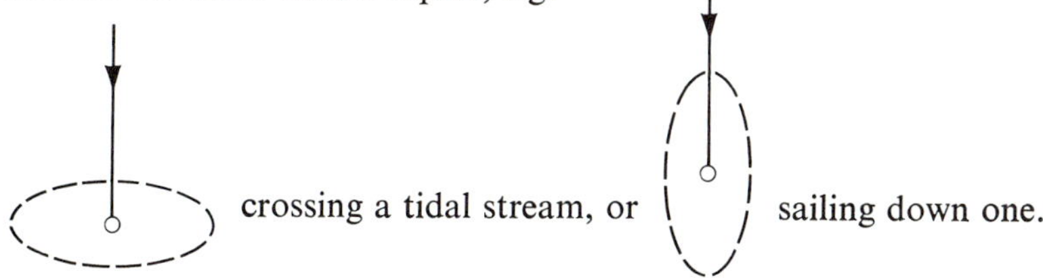

There are two reasons why I prefer these markings to the most widely recommended symbols. One is that the error circle or lozenge makes one think about the nature, extent and direction of probable errors. The second is that, by using a triangle for a fix, I can simply leave the cocked hat of a fix I have made; the dotted triangle reminds me that I can expect a fix at about that position and must try to get it. The real point I want to make, however, is that one system is as good as another, provided it suits the navigator and is understood by the whole crew.

Abbreviations for working logs

We shall be discussing logs just below, but here are a few ideas on symbols and abbreviations. First, on wind direction: even if you can box the compass (in my view a pointless act of recitation), your crew probably cannot; the 22°30′ points (NNE, etc.) are quite accurate enough for recording purposes.

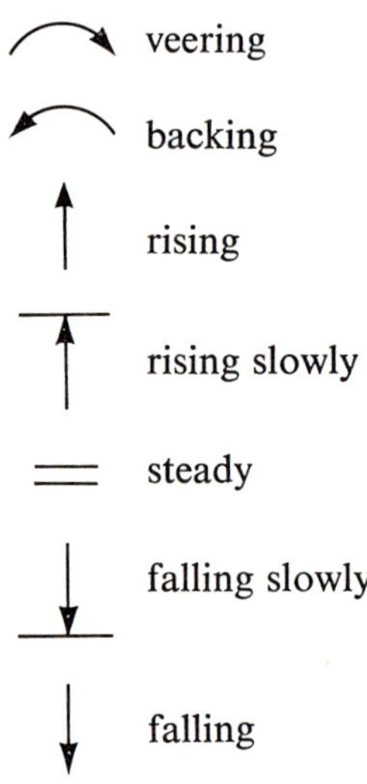

Working logs and log-books (see also page 44)

A lined exercise book or rough notebook of about A4 size makes an ideal *working* or *deck-log*. Don't rule columns, because you will sometimes need to make longish notes or do small calculations running across the page. But the main columns for normal entries are:

Date/Time	*Log reading (nm.)*	*Heading (°M)*	*Wind*	*Barometer*	*Event*
e.g. 121430A	15·23	280	SW4–5	1005	Tacked on to 200°M

(Incidentally, this entry should suggest to you that you may shortly have a Northwesterly gale on your hands and should be shortening sail and making alternative plans to turn and run.)

Such entries will be backed up by a corresponding note on the chart. In my view these entries should be related to *events, not to time* other than, for obvious reasons, just before or at a change of watch. (Ocean passages made under celestial navigation are of course a completely different matter.)

You must keep complete passage information for two reasons. One is that you must have a recorded datum to work back to if visibility closes down or something goes wrong. The second is that, if there is an accident, or a chartered or club boat is delayed or damaged, you must be able to give a full account supported by evidence of the events that led up to the incident. But once the passage is successfully completed, most of this detail is of no interest whatever. You can write up a short, amusing account in your log-book, note any new information either there or in the sailing directions concerned and then clean your charts and, if you wish, tear up your deck-log.

Chartroom facilities

In boats large enough to have a separate chartroom, the main cause of trouble is often the seat. This must hold you firmly in position on both tacks; it is very irritating to have to lash yourself in or use a harness when you are working at the chart table. The minimum facilities you need are:

1. A drawer or shelf to keep charts in; if this is elsewhere in the boat, you can probably keep working charts between the wooden top of the seat and the cushion.
2. A shallow drawer or such for instruments, pencils, etc.
3. A bookshelf that holds books firm but is easily accessible.
4. A hard flat surface, preferably with a raised edge, large enough to take an Admiralty chart folded once.

Many small modern boats have a dinette, and at night or on long passages the table is used to make up a berth. I have tried both using a portable board with the chart held on it by elastic, and standing up and wedging myself to use the galley worktop. Both are very awkward and in fact dangerous. The answer is to move one of the cushions of the dinette berth and use the table or a hard locker-top.

Perhaps the most important point about *chartroom lighting* (or the equivalent) is that it should not be in the helmsman's line of vision. Otherwise it will impair his reading of the compass and destroy his night adaptation, even if it does not dazzle him in the ordinary sense of the word. This is in fact one of the factors determining the position from which you navigate at night in boats without a proper chartroom.

Some people use a hurricane lamp or other paraffin lantern, suspended and turned well down, but I have a horror of these, particularly below-decks underway. You need a *chart light* on the boat's supply; these have a small head on a semi-rigid adjustable arm around 500–750 mm long and give a bright light on a small area. I also find a map-reading torch essential for using on the chart itself (see page 42).

Finally, it is absolutely essential to have facilities which allow you to use reference books and make plots in heavy weather. If a gale blows up, you may have to work out a completely new plan, or at least update and detail one of the contingency plans you should have made when planning the passage (Chapter 20).

11

Steering a Compass Course

We looked at the characteristics of steering compasses in Chapter 2 and again at the errors associated with them in Chapter 7. It will already be clear to the reader that his navigation can be no better than the ability of the helmsmen in the crew to steer a compass course. We saw that the deviation card could be a source of secondary errors in its composition and of mistakes in its use, and that it was greatly preferable to use a good compass and mount it where the deviation would not be significant.

Limits of accuracy

We also saw that the best the helmsman of a small yacht could be asked to do was to steer on a 5° or 10° mark or on a split 5° (i.e. 2°30′ or 7°30′) – e.g. 110°, 115° and maybe 112°30′ or 117°30′. The last two would be a subjective averaging between the two adjacent 5° units, i.e. 110° and 115°, or 115° and 120°.

A tactful, sensible navigator and an experienced helmsman can in fact go one better than this. The best way of steering a 2°30′ course is probably to think of it as half-way between the adjacent 5° units. Taking this argument one stage further, the navigator might say to the helmsman: 'I want you to split 110° and 115° but keep a bit towards 115° if anything. In other words I want about 114° if you can do it for me.' On the other hand the remarks of a particularly tolerant and genial friend of mine were entertaining rather than printable when he told me about an enthusiastic young navigator who brought him into the Solent on the wind to repeated cries of: 'You must hold ZERO ZERO ONE degree.'

This is what I mean by learning to live with errors. Another thing I always tell a helmsman when it applies, on the lines of my remarks on page 102, is on which side of the heading ordered I would prefer him to err. Sometimes of course this is a matter of safety, but I always like to be the right side of my desired course: up-wind and/or up-tide of it. Encouraged in this way a helmsman will often come back after a time or at the end of his trick and say: 'I reckon we'll finish up about 5° above that heading, 109–110° I mean instead of your 114–115°.' This you can allow for, at least mentally and probably on your plot, even adjusting course a little on the strength of it.

Sometimes a heading will involve a particular point of sailing that is dangerous (risk of gybing maybe) or uncomfortable and slow (quartering sea and jib not drawing). It is up to the skipper, the watchkeeper or the helmsman to point this out and for the navigator to respond. But a good navigator should be awake to this possibility and have a contingency plan. Good navigation means getting to your destination as quickly as you safely can. To allow a boat to roll about with bare steerage way on, foresails flapping and boom crashing in and out is not just bad seamanship; it is bad navigation too.

Picking a mark

We discussed the basic techniques of using a compass in Chapter 2. But whether or not you use the lubber-lines, it is not easy to keep a boat sailing well when you are steering with a wheel and have your eyes glued to a binnacle. It is doubly difficult with a tiller and a compass somewhere below it, because you have to lift and turn your head to see the sails and get the wind on your face. Quite apart from anything else, it means that a pair of eyes is making no contribution to keeping a lookout. It is tiring and boring for the helmsman, and uncomfortable for the rest of the crew because he cannot ride the sea properly.

On the wind, as we shall see in Chapter 17, it is best to sail by the sails and report your average heading to the navigator, who must then sort it out. Off the wind the helmsman should *pick a mark and steer on it*. There are three key points about doing this:

1. Make sure you are actually on course when you pick the mark by getting on course, choosing the mark and then *rechecking on the compass* that you are still on course.

2. Recheck frequently by a glance down at the compass.
3. Make a *major check every ten minutes or so*, depending on the conditions. If necessary pick a new mark or realign on your existing one.

All stars and planets except the North Star move round the sky quite fast enough to take you very badly off course if you head on one for an hour or more. Clouds too move across the sky. And because of coastwise tidal streams – the sea moving across the land, if you like – you cannot hold for long on a given navigation mark or landmark without going in a circle (Figure 20). Provided that the heading is rechecked often enough, navigation marks, landmarks, clouds, stars and lights are all perfectly adequate steering marks. The helmsman should choose one that is comfortable and gives him a chance to sail the boat properly and to keep a good lookout.

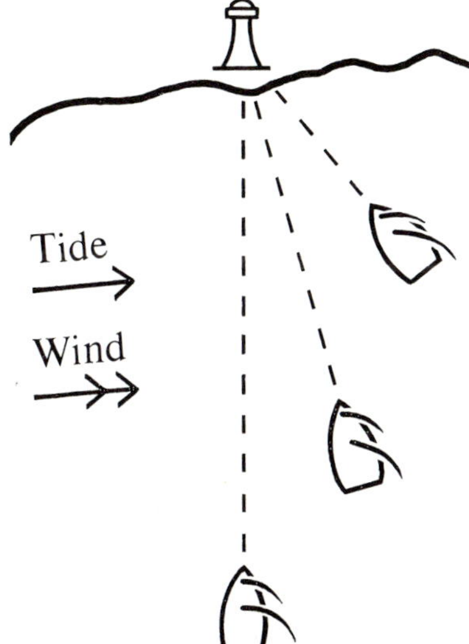

Figure 20. *Effect of holding too long on one mark.*

Often there are rather few good marks to be seen, but you can go on using the same one with an adjusted heading provided that you can find a way of relating the boat's heading to it (Figure 21). Note first that, if you are in a normal position for helming with a tiller, what appears to you as dead ahead (B) will in fact be fine on the starboard bow; if you steer to keep it on the stemhead or forestay

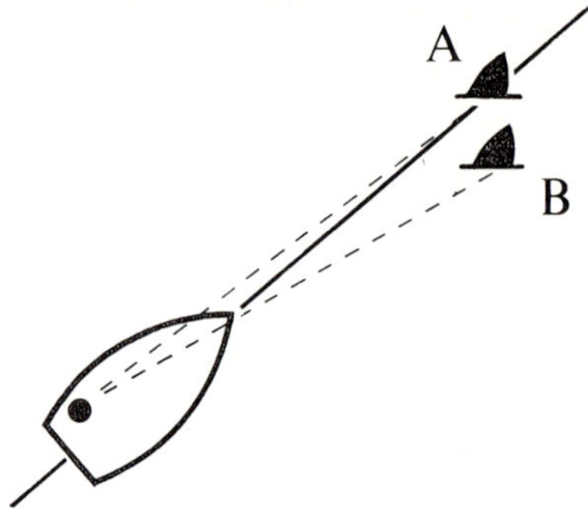

Figure 21. *Use of a single mark to steer various headings.*

you will go too far to starboard. A mark that *is* dead ahead (A) will be seen by you as fine on the port bow. This is in fact a large-scale example of *parallax*, mentioned in the context of instruments in Chapter 7. Pursuing this argument, you will see the possibility of establishing and holding a series of relationships with the same mark that will allow you to go on using it for a range of headings of 70° or 80° from one position of your head. Thus:

dead ahead
fine on the port bow
in the shrouds
(between forward lower
and forestay)
on port forward lower
on port main shroud
on port aft lower

(and the same on the starboard bow)

You can increase the scope further by standing on the centre-line of the boat, or, if vision permits, sailing her from the lee side.

Thus there is no moral or navigational merit in having a steering mark actually or apparently dead ahead. All you are doing is lining up the boat with the compass and then establishing a kind of rough transit between your eye, a sighting point on the boat (or a field between two vertical lines such as shrouds), and the mark. The need for frequent checks on the compass arises both because this is a rough-and-ready set up and because there will nearly always be some relative movement sideways between boat and mark.

Use of steering compass to take rough bearings

In the next chapter we shall be discussing fixes and the use of the hand-bearing compass to take accurate bearings. But this is a somewhat cumbersome procedure, and the helmsman can quite often get a rough bearing off the steering compass. Depending on the working position of the compass, the navigator may also be able to do this without disturbing the helmsman. Such bearings are often quite good enough for checking, for instance, whether you have reached a position where you should turn or tack, or whether you are making past the land over a foul tide. They are also useful in making a preliminary rough fix to decide which objects will give you the most useful set of angles for a proper fix.

Some say you can take a more accurate bearing in this way by using the lubber-lines, but in that case my own view is that you might as well use the hand-bearing compass held at waist level. To take a bearing with the steering compass, get your head in a position where your line of sight to the object runs over the centre of the compass card. (Imagine your line of sight to be the edge of a parallel rule laid on the rose on the chart.) Sight the object, then lower your eyes and note the compass reading you see in the centre of your field of vision and right way up, that on the far side of the compass from you. Don't forget that most compasses are marked in tens, so that '20' means 200°, with unnumbered marks for fives.

12
Bearings and Visual Fixes

The rates of tidal streams (Chapter 6) are often about the same as the speed of the boat through the water. Even within full sight of land, the need to tack, or to avoid or adopt a particular point of sailing may take the boat out of the area in which navigation marks can be used like sign-posts. And the problems highlighted in Chapters 8 and 9 in connection with losing and regaining sight of land also point to the need for means of finding the boat's position. This chapter and the next two discuss particular position-finding techniques; Chapter 16 draws them together and introduces yet another method – the use of soundings.

In Chapter 8 we noted how a transit – two fixed points in line, with your boat making a third – gave you a *position line*. You could plot on the chart a line passing through these two objects and say: 'I am somewhere along that line.' Suppose (Figure 22) that you are entering harbour on two lead marks, moving along a position line. If you now get, say, a beacon and a marked chimney in transit on the beam, you have established two *intersecting position lines* (B). You know your position: you have *fixed your position* or *taken a fix*.

There are just three snags. One is that you may have got the wrong chimney, or even confused one of the lead marks with another object, in which case you will not be where you think you are. You therefore need a third pair of objects, say a church and a tower on the headland behind you, to double check the intersection. What is more, these pairs of objects must be reasonably spread out so that you see a largish angle between them. If you had just the lead marks and the tank and windmill immediately to port of them, you could confirm you were on the right line but would have little idea where you were on it; the thickness of a pencil line might make a difference of several cables. Thirdly of course you will quite often be able to get one pair of objects in transit, but in real life the chances of finding two pairs simultaneously, let alone three, are negligible. Just as obviously, if you could work from three single objects instead of three pairs, you would be able to fix your position most of the time you are in sight of land or of navigation lights. You can do just this by *taking a bearing on the objects.*

Taking bearings

The instrument you use for taking visual bearings is the hand-bearing compass (see page 32). This has no magic advantage over other types of compass – simply that it is designed for the purpose and provided with a pair of sights.

Position

It was not until I reread the description of bracing yourself to shoot the sun in Mary Blewitt's *Celestial Navigation for Yachtsmen* that I

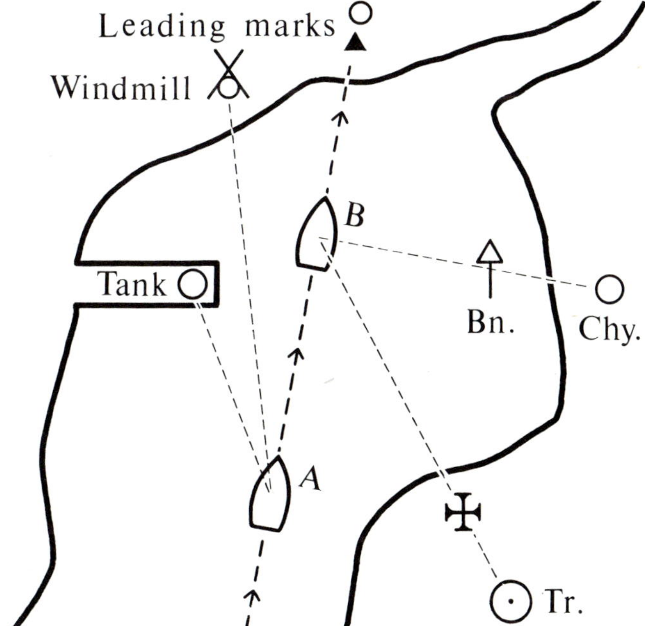

Figure 22. *Fixing position by transits (notional).*

realized why so many people cannot take fixes – they never get into a suitable secure position. It is necessary first to choose a position where the compass held up to your eye will be well clear of any mass of iron or steel, notably the motor. This distance needs to be at least 2 m, vertically, horizontally or on the slant. You must have the lanyard or strap of the compass on your wrist, so that there is no risk of losing that; and you should be harnessed and hooked on so that you need not worry about going overboard. Wedge yourself securely so that your body moves with the boat and the reflex movements of your neck and arm act as a kind of resilient mounting or gimbal. Make sure the compass prism is properly set and that you can hold it level at a distance from your eye at which you can read it.

In a very small boat there are usually two good positions. One is wedged in the doghouse with your head just below the line of the boom or above it if you are on a safe point of sailing and working to one side only. The other is sitting or half-lying on the fore-deck, probably harnessed to the mast, and looking out under the foot of the jib or over the weather side. In boats with a continuous line of steel formed by pulpit rail/lifeline/pushpit rail, it is desirable to hold the compass outside this, but the awkwardness of doing so may produce secondary errors.

Taking a series of bearings

Suppose in the ideal case (Figure 23) that you are making along a coast and have chosen three conspicuous objects roughly evenly spaced over an arc of around 150°. Try to take the three bearings quickly in sequence (say from bow to stern), allowing the compass just time to settle before reading it and moving on to the next. Blink, or wink your sighting eye between sights as you would in target shooting. If you cannot get a clear reading, don't wear your eye out. Lower the compass, rest your eyes for a few seconds and try again. You should take three such series of 'cuts' (readings); if you are unhappy about one cut or one series, discard it and take another.

Noting bearings

Like most other things, taking a fix goes much better with two; having to write each bearing or each series down as you take it is

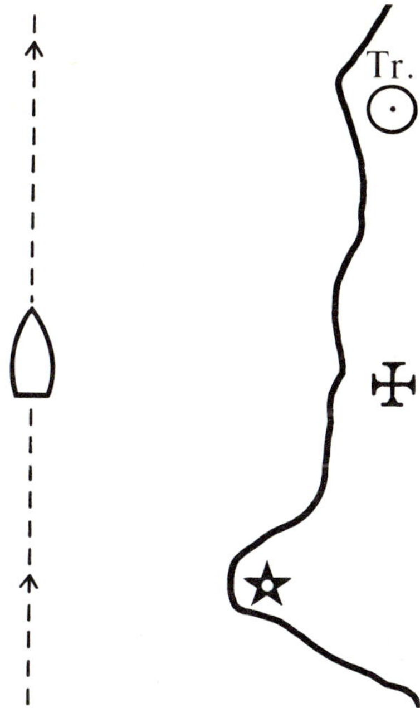

Figure 23. *Taking bearings (ideal case).*

time-consuming and leads to inaccuracies and mistakes. We discussed intercommunication and the importance of checking back in Chapter 4. Call the bearings as ZERO ZERO FOUR, ZERO NINE FIVE, ONE SIX FIVE, etc. The second person notes them (in normal figures) and calls them back one by one. This in fact gives you a very nice rhythm under reasonable conditions; it may even just about match the periods of the boat.

align – cut – call – turn and blink – (call back)
align – cut – call – turn and blink – (call back)
align – cut – call – turn and blink – (call back) – *end.*

Night fixes

The procedure by night is exactly the same, using the electrical or beta illumination of the compass (see page 32). After choosing the lights and identifying them on the chart and in your list or *Reed's*, go on deck and take a few minutes to reorientate yourself and regain a good degree of night adaptation before you take the fix. If you have to note the bearings for yourself, do so without looking down so as to conserve night adaptation; or close one eye as described below.

Night adaptation

We have mentioned night adaptation several times and this is probably a good point at which to explain it. In high light levels you see a thing best by looking straight at it, so that the image falls on the small central area of the retina (Figure 24) known as the *yellow spot* and formed of cells called *cones*. These cones, however, cease to respond when the light level falls to about the point at which you cease to perceive colour. The *rods* of which the rest of the retina is formed then take over. The amount of light admitted through the pupil by day would be too much for the sensitive rods, and they are in fact desensitized chemically when the eye is exposed to high levels of light. When the light level falls, a chemical known as *visual purple* starts to re-form in the rods and to restore their sensitivity. It builds up rapidly to begin with, but takes thirty minutes or so to reach its full quota. Night adaptation or night vision sensitivity depends on how much visual purple is present in the rods.

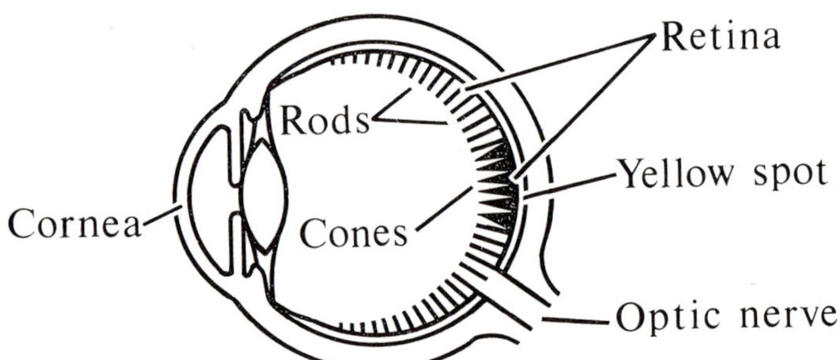

Figure 24. *Section through human eye.*

Visual purple is decomposed instantly by white light, and then takes its full time to build up again. If you have reasonably good vision in both eyes, you can close one to keep it night-adapted while you make a note or look down on the chart. Red light does not destroy visual purple; I have however tried using it in the chartroom and found it very difficult to work with on charts and small print.

You may think all this detail rather fussy and out of tune with the main lines of this book. But getting good visual fixes is by no means as easy as it looks; you are dealing with a fairly formidable set of errors. You therefore need to develop both systematic techniques for taking fixes and the knack of using the hand-bearing compass quickly and effectively by day and night, particularly in heavy seas.

Choice of marks

You may not have a choice of marks. You need three marks for the first and last fixes of a series; supplementary fixes can safely be made on two as a mistake will stand out, but it is just as quick to use three.

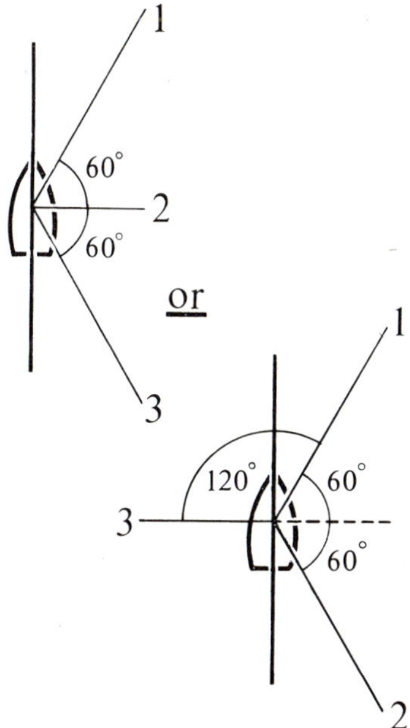

Figure 25. *Optimum angles for fixes.*

Still, two marks are better than one; and one, as we shall see below, is a bit better than none.

If you have a choice of marks, pick three at roughly 60° to one another (Figure 25) and give preference to ones which are really distinct and visible at long range, so that you can go on using them for a whole section of your passage. For various reasons, partly psychological, it seems to help if you can carry over at least one mark from one set to the next as you sail along the coast or through a channel.

If you make a landfall or beat in after a long board to seaward and are not quite sure where you are, it may be worth taking a quick series of cuts on all visible marks, noting their nature as well as their bearing, and then going down to the chart and trying to find a set of objects and hence a position that roughly fits your bearings. For this purpose and for other quick checks, it may be enough to use the steering compass (see page 121) or a wrist or pocket compass. Having found a rough position, you can pick your marks and take a proper fix. This procedure is much quicker than taking a proper fix only to find you have wrongly identified one or more marks or even (let's admit it!) that you are not on the stretch of coast you think you are.

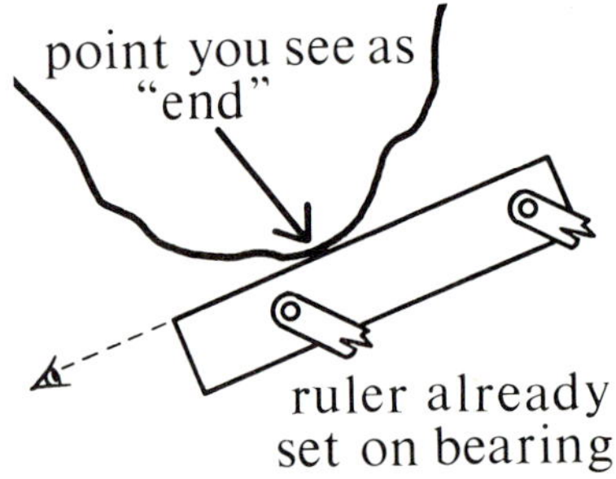

Figure 26. *Use of parallel rules to identify 'end' of headland.*

One tends to think of using navigation marks or buildings for fixes, but natural features are equally good. You can get a very clear cut on the end of a headland as you see it, and if you bring the rules across from the rose just to touch the coast, this will give you the point you see as the extremity (Figure 26).

Plotting a fix

First take an average of your three cuts on each mark. Spot the mean or, if the spread is wide and lopsided, add them up and divide by the number of cuts.

Work entirely on magnetic bearings and the magnetic ring on the rose. Use the procedure described on page 109, putting the rules first on the rose (through the centre!) and then walking them until one edge cuts the mark; then draw as much of the position line as you need. Incidentally, with some models of hand-bearing compass, it is fairly easy to read off the back-bearing instead of the bearing; if you use parallel rules and the magnetic rose (as opposed to a protractor), this does not matter.

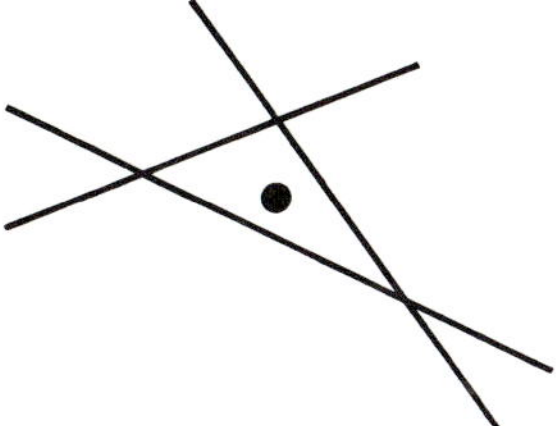

Figure 27. *Triangle of error.*

The three position lines will give you a *triangle of error* (Figure 27), and your position is considered to be *at the centre of this,* which you mark with a dot. There is a procedure for calculating the 'centre' of the triangle more accurately; but if the triangle is large enough to use it, you had much better get up on deck and take another series or two of bearings. On the other hand, if the three lines intersect at a single point, this is a good talking point but in fact a fluke.

You will see now that there are two quite separate reasons for taking three bearings whenever you can. One is that the 'cocked hat' *defines an area within which your position must lie.* If you had just two lines, you would not know which side of their intersection you were. Second, the use of three lines *shows up a mistake in the taking or plotting of one of the bearings.* In the first fix of a landfall you may not know which one or why, but you can see something is wrong and quickly sort it out. In subsequent fixes you will know your approximate position and so will be able to spot the mistake, especially if you are carrying a mark forward from one set of marks to the next.

If you get an enormous triangle of error or it does not close at all, clearly indicating a mistake, you may in fact be able to decide from other position-finding methods which bearing is probably or certainly wrong. Otherwise make sure that the least favourable intersection of any pair of lines (rejecting of course any that puts you back where you started or deep inland) does not put you in immediate danger. If it does, take the *minimum essential avoiding action* before getting down to a new fix.

Log only the essential data of a fix:

1. On the chart a △ with a time or date-time group and log-reading.
2. In the deck-log the usual entries and the bearings if it is a first or last visual fix; otherwise just time, log-reading and heading.

Tidal effects

In a coastwise passage when you are travelling basically parallel to the tidal stream, its actual rate at a given time and place may be very useful information. Armed with this you can interpolate in – or sometimes extrapolate from! – the figures given in the tidal atlas, and thus get a read of the whole tide. You will recall that we noted the log reading and time at each fix. We can measure the actual distance between two fixes off the chart, and the difference between this and the logged distance will give us the amount and direction of tide. We can express this in tenths of a knot as follows:

$$\text{Tidal stream in tenths of a knot} = 10 \times \frac{60}{\text{(time between fixes in mins)}} \times \text{(difference between measured and logged distances between fixes)}$$

We can now go to the tidal atlas and interpolate/extrapolate either by eye or by using the chart on the inside front cover (see page 76).

If you are crossing a tidal stream, the estimation of it is more complicated, but *precise* knowledge of the rate is much less important. The type of method needed for this estimation is discussed in Chapters 15 and 16.

Running fixes and single bearings

We said above that one mark is better than none; in a running fix, bearings are taken on one mark at intervals of time, as opposed to the 'simultaneous fix' described above, in which bearings are taken on two or three marks at the same time. I am going to stick my neck out and say that I do not consider the running fix a useful technique for the navigator of a small cruising yacht. I say this for four reasons. Since the technique is spread out in time, it is not easy to carry out in a small yacht on passage in a seaway, when various other things are going on. In waters with a significant tidal stream there is a vicious spiral of errors, with a bias tending to make you think you are safe when you are not. It is fairly rare, even at night, to have just one mark in sight; it is even rarer to need, for cruising purposes, the information you get from a running fix. (It is however a key technique when racing.)

I much prefer to use simultaneous fixes on two marks, taking immense care to double check; and I find it just as effective to use observation supported by single bearings when only one mark is visible.

I think however it is worth just outlining the principle of the running fix, because this will give the reader an insight into making rough checks with the aid of a succession of single bearings. Assume that there is no tidal effect and that wind force, sea state and point of sailing are such that you can steer the heading ordered accurately.

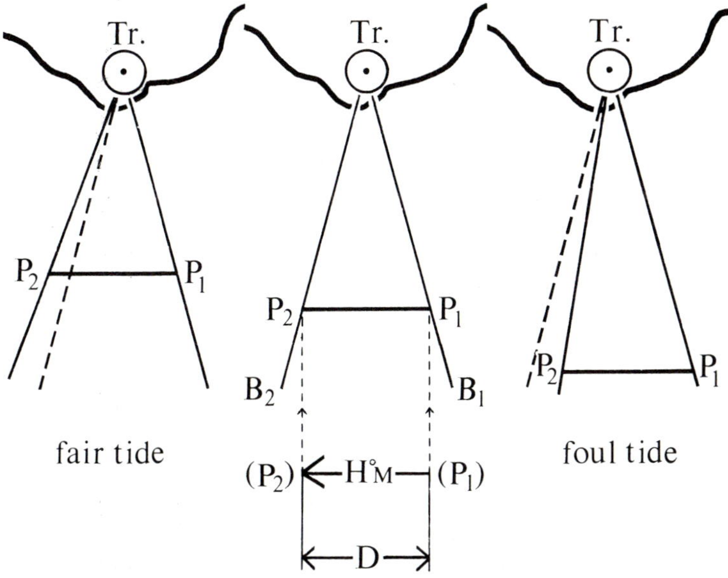

Figure 28. *Principle of running fix.*

Suppose (Figure 28) that at time T_1 the red beacon light on a radio tower bears B_1°M. You note the bearing, the time and the log reading. At time T_2, say 30 minutes later, the same mark bears B_2°M; again you note bearing, time and log reading. You know your heading (H°M) and the logged distance (Dnm.) between P_1, your position at T_1, and P_2, your position at T_2. Lay off a line, which we will call (P_1) (P_2) on your heading H°M and mark off distance D to the scale of the chart. Since the line (P_1) (P_2) is fixed in length and angle, there is only one way it will fit between the two bearing lines; this is at P_1P_2 – whence your positions. There is a very complicated geometrical method for establishing this line, but I usually do it by a series of approximations using dividers and parallel rules, alternately, or mark D in pencil on one edge of the rules and fiddle with it until I get it in the right place.

You will see the snag straight away. On a *foul* tidal stream, the distance past the ground will be less than D and your actual position will be *inside* P_1P_2. With a fair tide your will be outside P_1P_2, normally but not always the safe case. Laying off the tide on an unconfirmed tidal atlas figure over such a short distance is hopelessly error-fraught. If you really need to know exactly how far out you are, a running fix in a tidal stream is more likely to mislead you than to help you. It is much better to give yourself plenty of searoom, plot a desired course and take a bearing on the mark (maybe off the steering compass) every mile you log, or every quarter or half hour. You will then soon see if something is going wrong and you need to stand out.

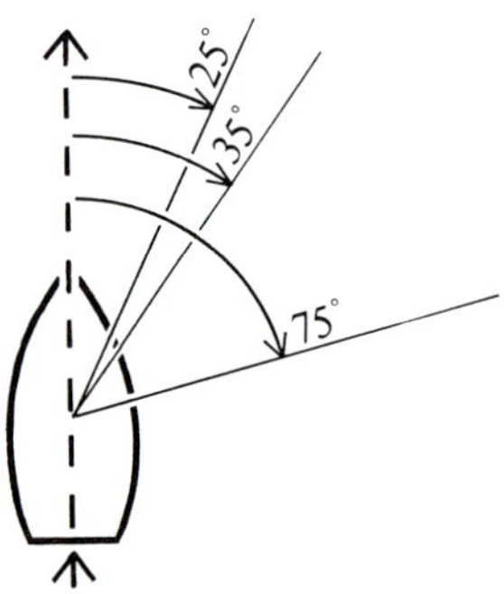

Figure 29. *Start angles for 'doubling the angle on the bow'.*

There is however one special case of the running fix that is useful, because it is very simple and can be done entirely by the helmsman without any plotting – in fact I would regard it as a check rather than as a position-finding technique. The procedure is known as *doubling the angle on the bow*. Suppose you are passing to port of a mark; it will first appear fine on the starboard bow and will then 'move round' until you finally lose sight of it on the starboard quarter. You can use the procedure starting at any angle off the bow between 25° and 75°, but to get the answer in time to take avoiding action you need to start at an angle between 25° and 35° (Figure 29). Watch the steering or hand-bearing compass until the mark bears 25°, 30° or 35° off the heading; then take and note the log reading. When the bearing has doubled (50°, 60° or 70°) note the log reading again. *Ignoring tidal effects and deviations from the ordered heading, the distance logged will be the distance off the mark when the second reading is taken. But remember above all that a running fix taken on a foul tide will show you as further out than you are; you must therefore allow an ample margin to clear a danger.*

13
Radio Fixes

We have seen that to take a good visual fix you need to have three marks in sight. There is no great mystery about a radio fix; the only difference between it and a visual fix is that the link between compass and known point is a radio signal and a special receiver instead of an optical image and your eye (Figure 30). You may even use the same mark, since most maritime *radio beacons* are also major lights in conspicuous positions. Thus when bad visibility forces you to abandon visual fixes or when you are out of sight of land and lights you have to resort to your *DF radio* (see page 35) to find your position.

Looking up and selecting radio beacons

You will find very full and useful information on radio beacons and other radio aids to navigation in Section XII of *Reed's*. We shall take as an example the first table, Channel Approaches to Noord Hinder under 'Radio Beacons Charts and Lists', Section XII. You also need *a single chart covering all beacons used and your own position*; this need to use a small-scale chart, such as No. 2675, *English Channel, Eastern Portion*, is one limitation on the accuracy of radio fixes.

On the left-hand page in *Reed's* you will see a sketch chart giving the positions of beacons, each of which is identified by a *station number*; this is an arbitrary number used by *Reed's* as a key. Now look at the table on the right. You will see the station number in the first column, followed by the name. The next two columns give the position, but in fact it is almost impossible to make use of a beacon in a small boat unless it is clearly marked on your chart. The fifth column gives the range in nautical miles, and the next the frequency (of which more in a moment). You will note that the beacons are 'boxed' into groups operating on the same frequency. It is convenient to work entirely off one group, but not essential; sometimes you get a better signal by choosing stations from two groups.

Suppose we are crossing from Le Havre to Poole. We shall try to work off the fourth group down, labelled CC (=Channel Centre). The notes 'bR' on the right apply of course only to the station they are opposite, in this case the Le Havre Light Vessel. Each station in the group has a two-letter Morse identification or *call-sign*. This group in fact contains an anomaly (which I learnt the hard way as usual!); Pointe de Ver is not 'ER' (··–·) but a local variant 'èR', è being ··–··. (The only list I know of these variants is the table on the preceding page of *Reed's*.) Finally we come to the transmission times. If you study these you will see that each station in a group is allotted one minute and they come up in turn. The basic cycle on which radio beacons are planned is six minutes, or ten transmissions per hour, although some operate continuously.

You will find it helpful to extract the names and call-signs of the group you are using (and of course any other stations you need) on to your working pad or deck-log.

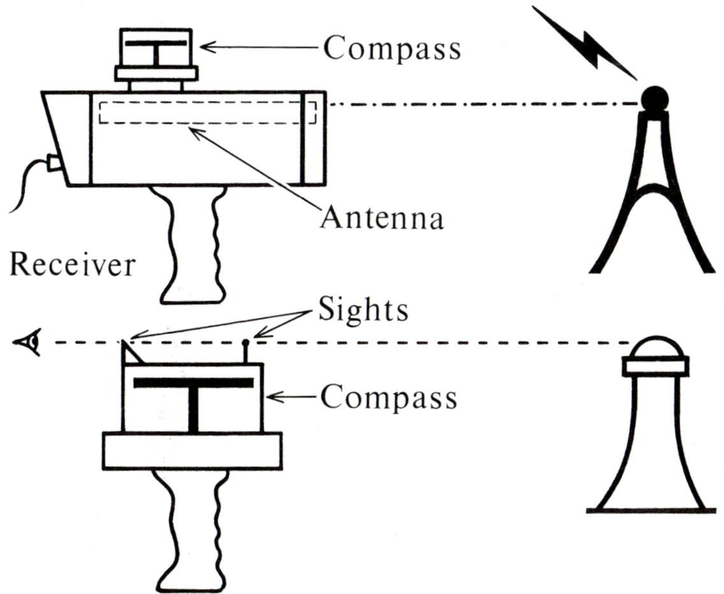

Figure 30. *Diagrammatic comparison of visual and radio fixes.*

Characteristics of signal

Within its allotted minute, the pattern of each signal is as follows:

Part	*Approx. duration* (secs.)	*Example* (St Catherine's Point)
Call-sign (repeated 2–6 times)	22	CP – · – · · – – ·
Continuous tone	25	(common to all)
Sign off with call-sign (once or twice)	8	CP – · – · · – – ·
Silent period, at least	5	(common to all)

Operating DF radio and establishing communication

Always use earphones or a 'stethoscope'; it is very difficult to use a DF radio accurately with a loudspeaker. The detail will vary slightly from set to set. Switch on and turn the gain (volume control) well up. Switch to the navigational mode ('NAV'). Set the tuning knob roughly to the frequency given, then search with it until you pick up a signal; listen for any call-sign or any letter in a call-sign of your group of beacons. Use the continuous note to fine-tune on, usually by turning the knob gently to and fro. You will hear a descending whistle as you move towards the correct point and a rising one as you move away; at the correct point you will hear only the basic signal. Don't mix this up with turning the antenna (see below); keep the set still while tuning. Once tuned, listen through the group once or twice, turning the set or the antenna to get the strongest signal for each station, and tick off on your list beacons from which you are getting the strongest and most regular signals. Choose the best three, or if possible four. Don't try to rush things unless you have been caught by fog. You should set up your DF radio for any passage which may take you out of sight of land, and whenever there is the least risk of reduced visibility.

Taking bearings

In Chapter 12 I mentioned the importance (for me at least) of establishing a rhythm when taking a series of cuts. This is even truer of radio fixes. The most accurate operator of a small DF set I know will sit for anything up to half an hour feeling himself in before starting to note bearings. When you are satisfied with your signals, wait for the weakest of the ones you are using and turn the *gain* DOWN *so that you can just hear its call-sign comfortably with the set/ antenna turned for the strongest signal for that station.* On the next cycle start taking bearings. Again of course you should keep the magnetic compass well away from masses of steel and the antenna well away from standing rigging. But a comfortable working position is probably even more important, especially if your stations are well spaced out round the compass.

Listen for the call-sign of the first station on your list to come up. As soon as you hear the continuous tone, turn the set (or the separate antenna) until the signal fades out – the 'null point'. Overshoot this and come back to it, 'bracketing in' like you did when tuning. When you are satisfied, read the compass and note the bearing. It does not matter whether you take the bearing or the back-bearing. If you are getting a good signal, you will be able to take two or three cuts on one continuous tone; these may vary by as much as 5°, so average them. Then repeat this procedure for the remaining stations. Use the gain control freely to make the call-sign audible and then to get a clear-cut null point. If possible, take bearings on four stations until you have been able to check a fix by other means.

Errors

From the moment of reading the compass onwards the error system is identical to that of a visual fix, apart perhaps from the problem mentioned earlier of having to use a small-scale chart. There are however additional errors in the radio stage of the procedure that tend to make radio fixes less accurate than visual ones and may be so large as to be positively misleading. Turning the radio or separate antenna to get a null point and identifying the null point has to be a less precise business than sighting on to a prominent object with a U and a bead. Secondly, the standing rigging can have an important effect. Apart from the need to separate the magnetic compass from iron or steel masses, there is a need to keep the antenna clear of the standing rigging with a separation distance of at least one-fifth of the length of the nearest stay.

In addition there are various phenomena which may 'bend the beam' by quite substantial angles. Twice, in an apparently ideal position for DF fixes, I have had a 16′ latitude difference in the positions indicated by two stations, while getting consistent and patently accurate longitude positions. One of these sources of errors is known as *land bend.* This is apt to arise if the line between the beacon and your position passes over land, particularly over high ground, or along a coastline. Examples might be: St Catherine's Point from the Solent, Barfleur or the Casquets heading south from Cap de la Hague, or the North Foreland from a position off Dover. Various forms of radio interference can also produce inaccuracies or even false readings. Another common source of error is tuning to a harmonic of the frequency; this will give you spurious bearings. Because of these radio errors you should work off four stations until you have confirmed a fix by some other means.

Confirmation by depth check

Ideally you should set up your DF radio while you are still working off visual fixes and confirm a radio fix with a visual fix. But even if feasible, this does not always happen; and the fact that you got a good radio fix while clearing Le Havre or off the Needles does not necessarily mean that your fix in mid-Channel, when you really need it, will be sound. The only ways you can get a fix from above are celestial navigation or prayer, both of which are outside the scope of this book. If you can see no lights or marks you cannot get one sideways. So there is only one way to go – down. Provided you have done your homework and established the height of water above chart datum (see pages 72–3), the soundings on the chart and the echo-sounder will usually give you a pretty good idea in which of two possible positions you are. In deep water the height above chart datum will not matter so much. (But don't forget that for the next few years your chart will probably read in metres and your echo-sounder in feet or fathoms!)

Homing in

Radio beacons in harbour entrances may sometimes be directional. In this case you will usually hear one Morse letter if you are off line to one side and its inverse on the other. You might for instance hear ALPHA (· –) to port of the leading line and NOVEMBER (– ·) to starboard. These signals are synchronized and superimposed; when you are on the correct approach line you will hear a continuous tone.

You can also home in on a non-directional beacon at a harbour entrance or on the approach to one simply by taking repeated radio bearings on it and aligning your heading to these. When doing this you must however remember to check on the chart that the bearing you are approaching on is a safe one. Cherbourg and St Malo are examples of this; Le Grand Jardin (St Malo) also exemplifies the second point.

14
Dead Reckoning

The methods of position-finding we have discussed so far depend on obtaining a fix, on finding one position at a given moment by reference to one or more fixed objects of known position. It makes no difference whether we use our eyes, a radio link or, in the case of depth checks, the reflected sound pulses of the echo-sounder, otherwise known as 'sonar'. In yachts fitted with it, *radar* in its simplest

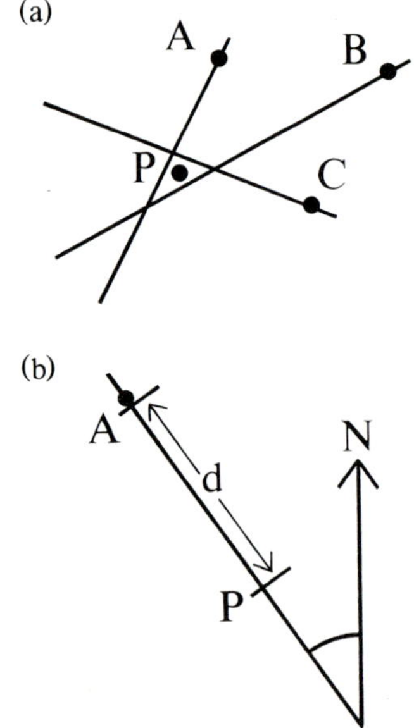

Figure 31. *Use of radar to obtain (a) bearings on three marks; (b) range and bearing on a single mark.*

form can be used in exactly the same way – to find the bearing of a series of objects and get a fix, just as if we were using a very powerful torch beam and our eyes (Figure 31*a*). I am not going into radar in this book because it is probably beyond the scope of most readers' pockets; but it does provide a useful link between techniques based on a number of known objects and those using a single one. For radar in its usual form gives the *range and bearing of a single* object (Figure 31*b*), which is another way of defining position. This is also the principle of one of the most ancient methods of navigation, *dead reckoning*. The difference is that with radar you can get the range and bearing of a point A after you have left it; *in dead reckoning you have to measure distance and bearing, or rather heading, continuously.*

Principle of dead reckoning

I first learnt dead reckoning in the North African desert, where one would set out from, say, a surveyed well with a map often blanker than an ocean chart, a device known as the sun-compass (in effect a sundial adapted to give heading from a time input), a watch and the mileage recorder, or if you must, odometer, of a vehicle. I mention this not just for the sake of reminiscence but because it makes three basic points about dead reckoning:

1. You must start from a known point marked on the chart, the *datum point.*
2. Dead reckoning assumes that you are moving in a straight line and that the medium you are moving in or on is stationary with respect to the known point. *Dead reckoning take no account of yaw, sideways displacement or tidal stream.*
3. You require a means of maintaining and/or measuring heading, *the steering compass*; and a device for measuring distance travelled, *the log.*

You can use dead reckoning not just for a single course, but for a series of 'legs', provided you note the heading of each leg and the log reading at the end of it. In still water you could start from a known position A, say a buoy, sail a hexagon of 1 nm. side and back to A, provided that you noted the log reading and heading at each turn (Figure 32).

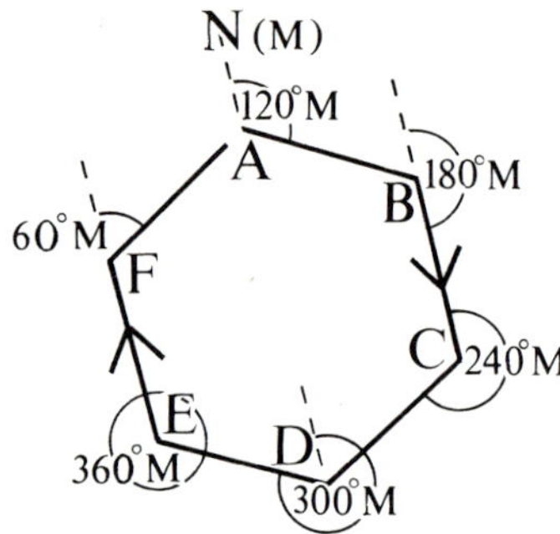

Figure 32. *Sailing a hexagon by D R.*

Point	*Heading*	*Log reading*
A	120°M	0·0
B	180°M	1·0
C	240°M	2·0
D	300°M	3·0
E	360°M	4·0
F	060°M	5·0
A	(finish)	6·0

Likewise you can plot this on the chart.

The log

We discussed the various types of log and their problems in Chapter 2. I shall deal in this chapter with the Walker Knotmaster K D O log, probably the best known form of the 'patent' or trailed log (Photo 6).

Setting up

The plate permanently fixed to the deck, known as the *shoe*, must be in a position where the log line will run clear out astern and where the main instrument or *register* can be easily mounted, dismounted and read. Ideally one should have a shoe on either side; make sure they are the right way round, so that the pull of the log line tends to hold the mounting locked, not to undo it. Also use a securing lanyard in case you drop the register or it works loose and dismounts itself. Sling mountings for suspending the register from the pulpit are available for some types of log.

Each time you dismount the register, *zero* it by opening the front and turning each hand *anti-clockwise* to zero; or by using the knob provided. When you mount the register, double check that it is accurately zeroed.

In the Walker log at least, the outer (aft) end of the central hole in the rotator (i.e. the end where the blades are widest) is specially shaped to accept the knot the instructions tell you to tie in the end of the line. If you use a knot of a different shape, the rotator can spin on the line.

Maintenance

If you do not look after your log, it will become stiff to turn and the errors which are unavoidable at low speeds will extend to moderate speeds. Use either special log oil or a top quality machine oil (such as Three-in-One); some oils form a frothy mixture with salt water, and this is disastrous. Use enough oil to act as a waterproof seal as well as to lubricate the mechanism. Most registers have an oil-hole in or near the face, but a lot of people do not realize the importance of lubricating the main bearing by dropping oil down past the hook. When oiling or zeroing, drain out any water that has got inside the log, and wipe the outside clean and dry. Then make sure the cover-retaining screw is fully home and tight.

Streaming the log

This means putting the line out. Clear away the line; lay the sinker and rotator out separately and the line itself loosely coiled on the cockpit seat or, if safe, on the deck. Grasp the plastic eye on the line firmly, check that it is securely attached to the line and hook it on to the rotating block in the back of the register. Pull it outwards firmly but not violently to make sure it is properly hooked on. Then, starting with the end nearest the hook, slowly pay out the line over the stern so that it forms a bight on the surface well clear of the screw and rudder. Finally pick up the sinker and rotator, give the line another little tug just behind the hook to make sure it is attached, and then throw the rotator and sinker diagonally aft and to one side. The line will be drawn straight and taut and will start to rotate: recheck that it is clear of all parts of the boat.

Reading the log

On the Walker log you have a large hand for tens of miles, one small hand for unit miles and another small hand for tenths of a mile or cables. *Use all three hands when you take a reading*, taking one figure from each; then you will get it right, e.g. Big hand ONE, mile hand THREE, cable hand SEVEN = 13·7 nm.

Handing the log

This means getting the line in. Do this in good time before entering harbour so that someone can give it their full concentration. If you do it wrong by simply pulling the line in, you will get the line in a tangle and may fray it. If you do it right, it is fairly easy to lose it over the stern. Grasp the line *very firmly* just astern of the hook, holding the eye with your finger and thumb. Move the eye forward, sideways and back to disengage it, *keeping a firm grip*. Pass the eye round the pushpit rail or a backstay and let it fall or trail astern. Pull in enough of the main length of line to get the eye 'streamed' into the sea. Then pass the line smoothly but firmly through your hands until you are holding the rotator and the eye is trailing astern. Put the rotator and sinker down inside the cockpit and recover the line, giving it time to straighten out in the water, and loosely coil it to dry. When dry, hank it up and stow it in the box very carefully.

Log errors

We noted in Chapter 2 that most types of log read low at very low speeds, and explained how to minimize this effect by using only one sinker, or none at all, and a half-length line. For faster boats, you really need two lines ready fitted with eye, sinker and rotator, one being about twice the length of the other. It may also sometimes help to move the sinker a few centimetres further from the rotator at low speeds. If the line twists and bunches itself with the register not moving and suddenly unwinds and makes the register spin violently, you are going to get inaccuracies. You must keep the 'stiction' (breakaway friction) of the register as low as possible by regular and correct oiling.

On the other hand it would be wrong to assume that your log is virtually not working because the line hangs deep in the water and turns only slowly and intermittently. Under these conditions it will read low enough to give you a significant error, but *never low enough to justify your wildly optimistic predictions of position*!

Speed checks

If you do not have a speedometer, and there is little need for one in a small cruising yacht, you can find out your speed quickly and accurately with the log and a stop-watch. The time over five cables will give you a reasonable figure. Or take three readings over one cable each and average them. With a good breeze and a moderate sea, checks like these are quite accurate enough to trim your sails to. Also of course note the distance travelled each hour and/or between fixes, and calculate speed from this.

Establishing datum position

To get good results from dead reckoning, you must zero the log correctly and stream it at an absolutely unmistakable position, such as a transit at the harbour entrance or an outer channel marker. Any confusion over this position or the log reading at it makes the whole technique meaningless. Taking the log reading at a firm visual or radio fix establishes secondary datum positions.

Plotting and logging

To work off dead reckoning, you must note in the deck-log:

1. The position, log reading and time of streaming the log.
2. The initial heading.
3. The log reading at each fix, and any change of heading.
4. The log reading and new heading at each tack or change of heading.

To make a dead reckoning plot on the chart, you simply use the parallel rules to draw a line representing your heading through your last known or estimated position, lay the length of the leg off with dividers and mark your new estimated position with a circle or whatever mark you use, the letters DR, and a time.

Because of tidal effects and the fact that your boat does not always sail in a straight line down its ordered heading, this will rather seldom be your actual position. That is why your last visual fix before losing sight of land and your first visual fix after a landfall (Chapter 12) are so important; and why radio fixes (Chapter 13) in between are useful even in clear weather. In the next two chapters we shall draw all of these methods together, first to find out where we have actually got to, and then to get to where we want – or very near it.

15
Position-Finding

In the early part of the book I laid great stress on double checking data. This is basically because you can live with errors but you may die from a mistake. Exactly the same applies to the problem of knowing where you are, which is the subject of this chapter; in the next we shall look in similar terms at the art of predicting where you will be or, on the other side of the coin, of getting where you want to go. In the last few chapters we have examined the various ways of following a chosen course, or conversely of finding one's position, and seen how these complement and dovetail into one another. It is quite true that you can usually sail around in sight of land in well-charted and -marked waters just by pilotage (Chapter 8). Equally, you will be in a very embarrassing position if fog suddenly comes down unless you are not just geared to use another technique but also have it, so to speak, running on standby and ready to go into action immediately – rather as you do the engine when you are making a difficult entrance under sail.

Before we go deeper into this, let me put before you one aspect of the paradox which to my mind lies at the root of good navigation; its other aspect belongs to the next chapter. *Unless you have an absolutely firm datum or reference position to work from, you cannot navigate with any accuracy. On the other hand, once you have a new firm position fixed, charted and logged, everything that happened before is irrelevant.* To illustrate this with the Poole–Cherbourg example used earlier, you close Poole Bar buoy and stream your log; this is a datum. You then get two good fixes on the lights of Anvil Point, the Needles and St Catherine's Point; you plot and log these, noting your log reading. Poole Bar matters no more. Some hours later you get a fix on the looms of Barfleur and the Cherbourg main light; this is useful but not good enough. After a while you pick up the Cap de la Hague light as well and get a nice tight cocked hat. You chart and log this. Then it matters not the least whether you have come straight across from Poole, up from Dartmouth, down from Le Havre or for that matter dropped out of the sky.

The datum position

If you close and positively identify a charted mark, note your log reading and set a compass course, you have a firm datum position for dead reckoning (Chapter 14) and corrections from it. Most people regard a three-point visual fix (Chapter 12) on positively identified marks as an acceptable datum. I do not. I prefer to treat this as a secondary reference position until I get a second independent fix on the same marks and both the position of the first fix and the position of the second fix relative to it tie up with the dead reckoning data. Then I am prepared to take the second fix as a datum and forget everything that happened before it. I would however never use a radio fix (Chapter 13) even if confirmed by a depth check (see page 138) as a primary dead reckoning datum; both the error zone and the risk of a mistake are too great. On the other hand a radio fix is a great help and a useful secondary reference.

This distinction between a primary reference or datum position and a secondary reference position is not a quibble. You can work from a secondary reference and it will often be quicker and easier – and therefore generally more accurate and reliable – to do so. But you must keep the deck-log, the plot and any other data sources in a form that will allow you to work back to the datum and forward again from it if you need to.

Timing of log entries

Do not be led by the conventional layout of log-books (see page 44) or by conventional teaching into making a log entry every hour on the hour. For inshore and coastal work and short offshore passages this is meaningless. You need to log each piece of navigational data as soon as you acquire it and each nautically relevant event as it happens. If tide and wind are playing up or you have to take avoiding action in a busy entrance channel or shipping lane, you may need a log entry every five or ten minutes to keep track of where you have been and hence of where you are. In particular you must log tacks. In a tricky passage such as Cherbourg to St Peter's Port through the Alderney Race you need to fix at least every half-hour.

On the other hand a one-tide passage along a coast you know well calls only for pilotage, with the log streamed and an idea of heading and/or distance off the shore or a mark in case visibility suddenly closes down. Even then you cannot afford to be too casual. Not long ago I was reaching gently down in sunshine about two miles out, with a prominent landmark on the starboard bow and approaching a very familiar entrance. We had seen one 'wintry shower' pass astern of us. Then one hit us; suddenly visibility was down from 15 miles or so to 50 yards and the wind up to Force 7 gusting 8. Although we knew where we were, we had to heave to to avoid getting downtide of the entrance before we could see to turn into it.

Passages of 150 nm. or more without sight of land or marks are quite a different matter. Then everything settles down into a routine, and one is going to use radio fixes and/or celestial navigation. Hourly navigational activity of some kind, even if only plotting the latest DR position, becomes a useful discipline. But whatever you do, you must always be ready to estimate your position at any moment, in case you either witness or suffer an emergency.

Celestial navigation

Having mentioned celestial navigation, I should perhaps try at this point to put it into perspective. Celestial navigation is the technique of finding your position from observations of heavenly bodies. Its purpose apart, it bears virtually no relation to the techniques of pilotage and short-range navigation which are the subject of this book. Although celestial navigation is a very precise art, the size of some components in its error system is substantial. For instance, a second of time is the equivalent of a nautical mile. Thus positions obtained by these techniques, particularly by amateur navigators working in small-boat conditions, tend to have an error zone of tens of miles. In the middle of the ocean, knowing your position to within say 25 miles is an immense asset and provides a useful check on several hundred miles of dead reckoning. In the Thames Estuary or Channel Island waters it is useless, because half a mile is the difference between deep water and a sandbank or a rock.

The instruments used in celestial navigation are a chronometer and a sextant. The documentation consists of tables, which you will find for instance in Sections II–V of *Reed's*. Basic celestial navigation is not in fact as difficult as the documentation makes it look; someone well versed in the techniques covered in this book would probably find celestial navigation about as difficult a subject as the contents of this book are for the dinghy sailor.

Drift

A boat sailing off the wind at moderate speed in calm, still water should in fact follow her dead reckoning course precisely. Chapters 6 and 7, and much else in this book, will have left the reader in little doubt that this rather seldom happens. Suppose (Figure 33) we close a conspicuous, identified mark and then steer a compass course for 45 minutes, giving a DR position E. Then we take a visual fix putting us at F. Suppose also that there are no mistakes or abnormal errors. We have first to explain the distance EF and then to analyse it. This distance EF is known as the *drift* – in my view a very bad name but one so widely used that it must be accepted.

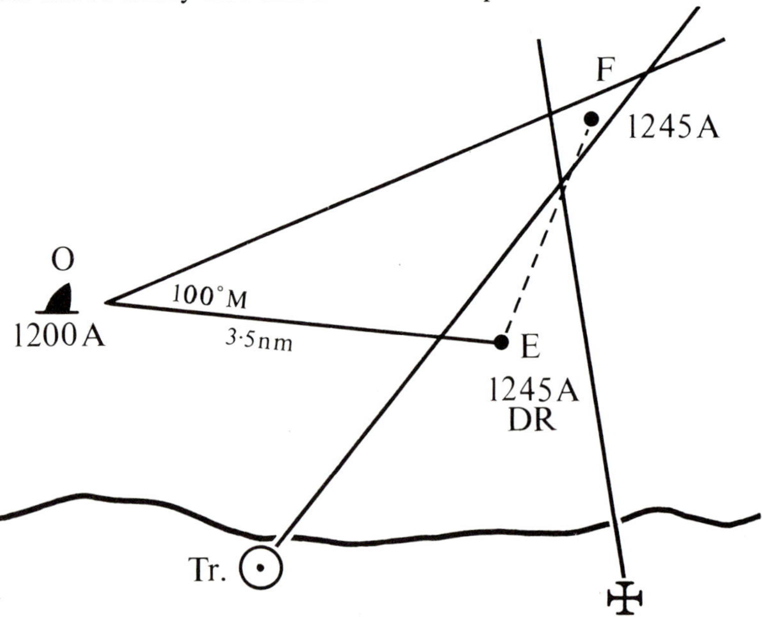

Figure 33. *Difference between DR and actual position.*

Broadly speaking there are *four components* in this drift. In smooth, still water we should expect (Chapter 7) a *small* difference between E and F, just as we should expect a cocked hat round F rather than a point intersection. This difference comes from the *random errors* of the two-position-finding techniques, dead reckoning and taking bearings, together with the associated plotting errors. In any particular instance, the difference may lie in any direction and may be of any magnitude from zero to a calculable '99 per cent' value. With the resources at our disposal we have no way of finding out more about it.

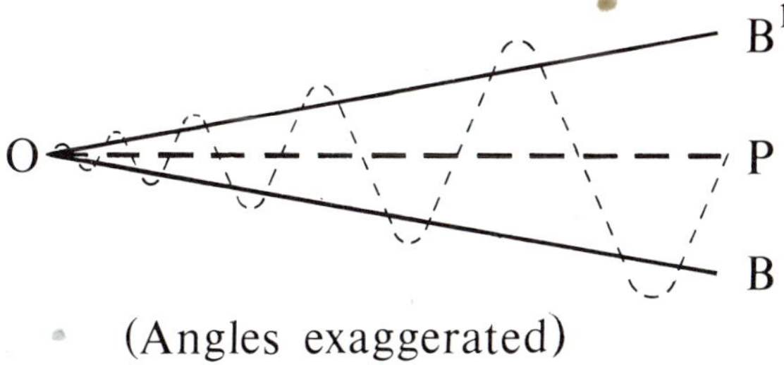

Figure 34. *Steering error.*

The second component is *steering error*. We know (see pages 89 and 117) that the heading given on the compass may not coincide with that ordered, and that helming in a seaway involves a sort of subjective averaging. Thus we have another quite complex *random error system* (Figure 34). This does not look like a random system but it is one. We do not know how large the error angle BOB′ is nor (although one must draw it one side or the other) do we know which side of B B′ lies. We certainly do not know the magnitude of B′OP; nor do we know the direction of it (unless the helmsman can give an indication – see page 117. Above all we do not know whether BOB′ and BOP are in the same direction and compound one another, or whether they cancel each other out.

The third component is *sideways movement of the boat through the water*. Traditionally leeway was treated as a known error or 'bias' and allowed for by laying off a leeway angle. Having sailed a shallow-draught junk I can see why. But with modern rigs and hull forms properly handled I believe that this lateral component is not just too small to allow for deliberately, but that, where it does arise, the net effect is just as likely to be to windward as to leeward (Chapter 17).

I must confess – and this is just what I mean by using the seat of one's pants rather than a pocket calculator – that in a boat I know being sailed by people I know, taking account of conditions and point of sailing as well, I fudge my drift correction a fraction one way or the other. This makes me feel good and may sometimes even bring the boat a shade nearer the best heading. The one exception to all this is sailing reefed right down in heavy weather with the wind forward of the beam; then I would expect to allow at least 2° or 3° leeway. But normally this lateral movement is another random error and there is nothing we can know or do about it other than sail the boat properly.

We are left then with the fourth and by far the most important component of drift – *the movement of the water past the land*, in other words *tidal stream*. This is something whose strength and direction we can estimate with fair accuracy from our documentation (Chapter 6). It is also something we may need to know precisely for a particular tide if we are faced with a tricky passage. Since we are concerned in this chapter with confirming our position, let us pick up the second of these points.

Use of drift to obtain accurate tidal stream data

In Chapter 12 we noted that a fair or foul tide would cause a difference between the distance logged between two fixes and the actual distance between them. This difference could be used to calculate tidal stream rate at a given time and place. Armed with this we could go into the tidal atlas and get accurate rate figures for the whole tide. The assumption here was that our boat's heading was roughly parallel to the tidal stream – as of course it would normally be in a coastwise passage (Figure 35*a*).

Suppose we now simplify and slightly exaggerate Figure 32, ignoring all causes for the difference between E and F except tidal stream (Figure 35*b*). O was a datum position. We have sailed through the water from O to E but arrived at a position F with respect to the land. In the simple case covered on page 150 and represented in Figure 35*a*, we had no doubt that E′F′ represented the movement of the water past the land during the 45 minutes in question. Clearly EF in Figure 35*b* must represent just the same thing. In both cases, if the sketches represent plots to scale on the chart, we can prick off E′F′ and EF with the dividers, measure them on the latitude scale and calculate the tidal stream rate.

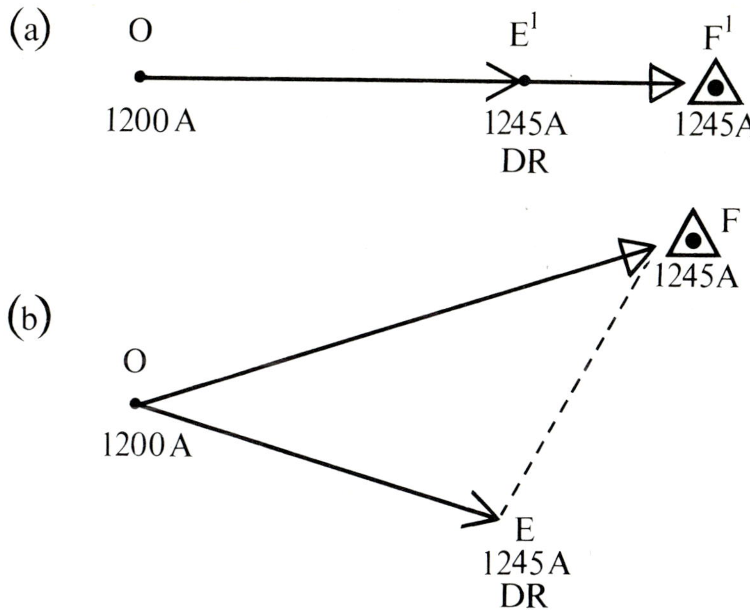

Figure 35. *Determination of tidal stream from drift: (a) heading parallel to stream; (b) heading oblique to stream.*

Opposed as I am to convention in whatever context, I should like to burden the reader with a few small conventions here. The line OE is known as the *course*; it represents the length and direction the boat has moved through the water between 1200 and 1245 hours. Since we are treating all components of drift bar tidal effect as random, OE coincides with the *heading* or *course steered.* EF represents the *drift*, in this case tidal stream. Since OE and EF together make up our movement relative to the land, they are called 'components' and are shown with an open arrow-head when we plot them. Note also that the arrow on OE 'runs up EF's tail'.

OF is known as the *track*; it represents the distance made good past the land, or if you prefer it, over the sea bed. It results from both OE and EF, so it is called the 'resultant' and shown with a closed arrow-head when we plot it. Note also that the closed arrow-head on OF *opposes* the open arrow-head on OE. In the next chapter we shall be using a similar method to predict headings and estimate future positions. These conventions help to avoid the disastrous mistake of getting drift the wrong way round!

16

Determination of Heading and Course Planning

In the last chapter we examined drift and decided that, apart from an occasional bit of fudging based on subjective judgement, we could really treat drift as a single error – or correction – considering only the component arising from tidal effects. The other components of drift are normally random or can be treated as such; and this approach gains force when we look back to Chapter 7 and see that these components are of the same magnitude as the other errors small-boat navigators have to live with. We first looked at drift from the point of view of explaining the difference between a dead reckoning position and one confirmed by a visual fix. Now we shall tackle the problem of working out the heading needed to cover a given *track* (movement relative to the land).

Safety margins

Chapter 10 highlighted the need to plot a predicted position as an error circle or lozenge rather than as a point. Since one is estimating subjectively the net effect of a bunch of random errors the estimate, even if correct probability-wise, may still differ rather widely from the event. Any rule of thumb must be tempered by common sense, but I should allow a safety margin of at least four times my estimated error between my expected position and any danger. In this case one must count completely missing the landfall as something nearly as serious as a danger (Figure 36). In (*a*) I would turn at P′ at the very latest unless I could get a fix. You will appreciate how strong the temptation to stand on might be if I was beating and trying to fetch a mark or clear a danger on the next board. And in (*b*) I would 'aim' at least 4 nm. *west* of the headland with the lighthouse, even if this could run me into problems of getting downwind or downtide of my objective.

Estimation of drift

Treating tidal effects as the sole or at least the overriding factor in drift, we can find the direction with some accuracy from the tidal atlas and get a good first approximation of rate from tidal atlas and chart (Chapter 6). In many waters we must then apply a correction factor to the rate to take account of conditions. In fact we can make a provisional plan and use the early part of the passage to improve the accuracy of the rate figure; this was discussed on pages 130 and 152–3.

In the previous chapter I mentioned one aspect of a paradox which underlies much in navigation – and for that matter in other sports which involve an element of risk to life. Let me now introduce the other aspect. *You must make a careful and precise plan in advance for each leg and for the passage as a whole. But you have got to be ready*

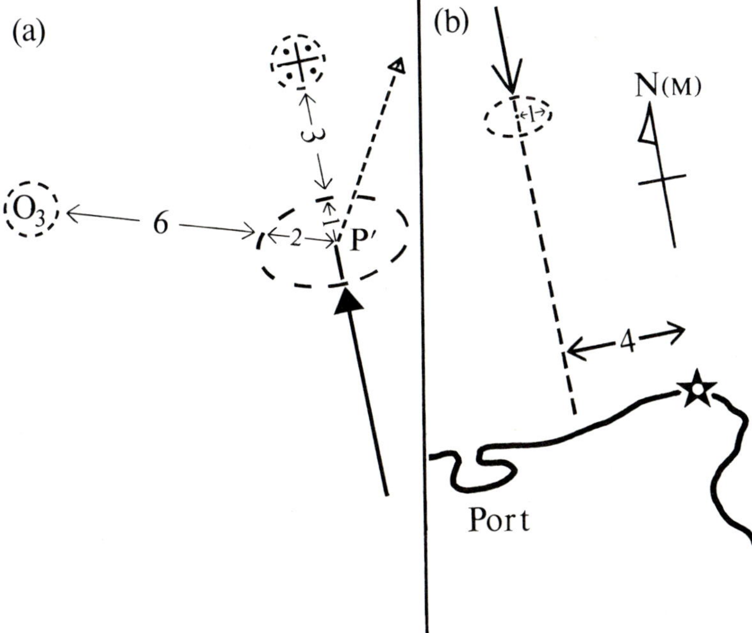

Figure 36. *Safety margins: (a) to clear dangers; (b) to achieve a landfall.*

to tear it up and start again when timings or conditions change or when you manage to improve your data.

Suppose for instance you intend to open the coast obliquely, and that you have calculated your first seaward leg on a tidal stream of 1·2 k. You clear harbour and set course, and a couple of quick fixes and your log tell you that the rate is in fact around 1·7 k (see pages 152–3). You are going to have to order a new heading straight away, and then to recalculate the tidal stream rate for the whole of that tide and replan accordingly.

Estimation of speed

To get the speed problem into perspective you need to bear in mind that tidal stream rates are roughly the same as the speed of small cruising yachts; so an error in speed estimation is not going to be all that disastrous. Once again I am going to stick my neck out. For planning I think one can consider a four-speed boat rather like a four-speed gearbox:

1. Steerage way plus.
2. Normal speed with wind abaft beam.
3. Normal speed with wind forward of beam.
4. Near Froude formula speed.

For my present boat these speeds might be:

1·5 k, 3·5–4 k, 5 k, pushing 6 k.

For a larger boat with more sail area and a hotter hull form, perhaps:

2 k, 5 k, 7·5 k, pushing 9 k.

Looked at this way, the problem reduces to two questions with 'yes/no/don't know' answers:

1. Will there be enough wind to get us sailing properly?
2. Will the wind force us to shorten sail and/or will the sea state slow us down?

If the answer is 'don't know', you have to make two plans. In any event you will have to make a heavy-weather plan, and that covers 'yes' and 'don't know' for the second question.

Provided you get in the right parish this very crude approach will give a speed estimation error of around the same magnitude as the probable tidal stream prediction error. Once again the distance logged and the time interval of your first two fixes will give you a much firmer figure on which to refine or modify your plan.

Determination of heading for a given track

A first hidden assumption here is that *you know where you want to go.* 'Going out for a sail' is a navigator's nightmare. A second assumption which we have discussed at some length is that *you know where you are.* For the moment we shall make a third: that a straight line drawn on the chart between the two shows a passage clear of dangers by an adequate safety margin, so that there is only one leg. To make things simpler, let us start from the mark O at which we stream the log and take as our objective a mark P, 20 nm. away (Figure 37).

First draw a line between the two marks (1); this is your *desired track. Take drift first,* because it is outside your control and fairly accurately known. *Work hour by hour.* Look up the tidal rate figure in the tidal atlas, check and refine it from the chart if you can and

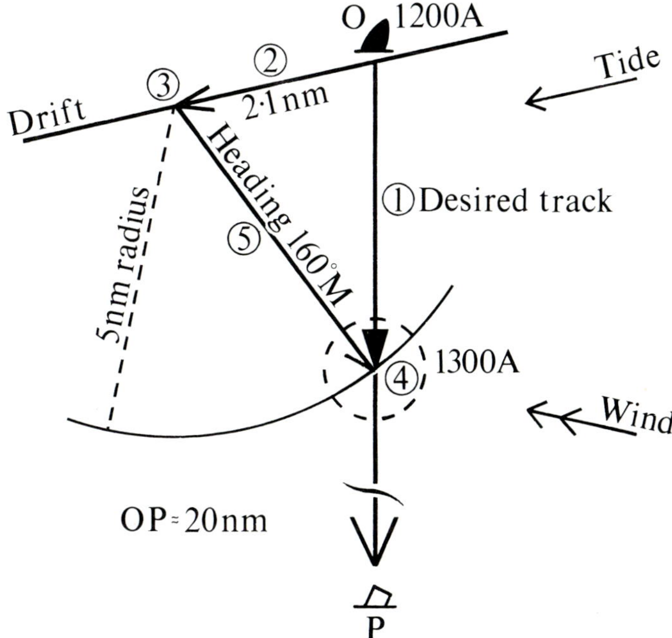

Figure 37. *Determination of heading.*

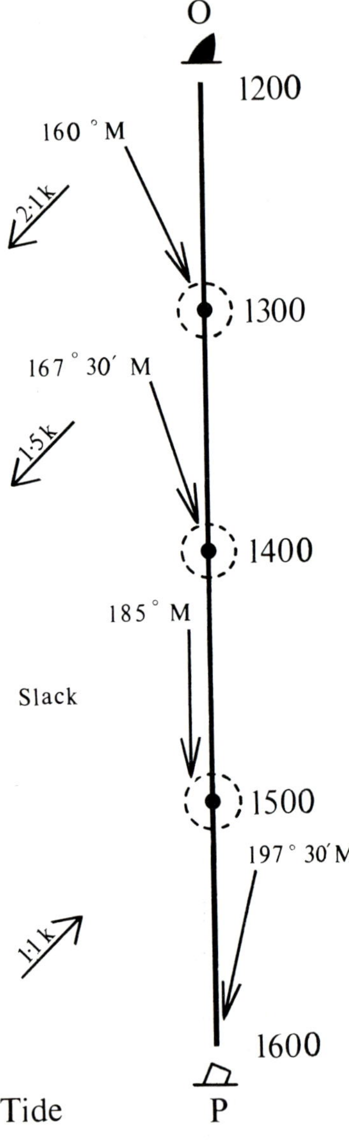

Figure 38. *Headings diagram for 20 nm. leg O P.*

adjust it a bit subjectively if you have any reason to. Suppose you end up with 2·1 k. *Lay off a line through O* parallel with the direction of the tidal stream as shown in the atlas (2). *Measure off 2·1 nm.* with the *dividers* on the latitude scale and mark off this distance from O *in the same direction as the tide* with an open arrow-head (3). This arrow-head represents the position where you would be after an hour if you literally drifted from O, that is if you remained stationary in the water.

Now estimate your likely *speed*; using my rule of thumb above, say 5 k under the given conditions. Take the *compasses* and set them on the latitude scale to a radius of 5 nm. (5 knots = 5 nm./hr). With centre at (3) *strike an arc* to cut the line OP (4); join (3) to (4) and put an open arrow-head. Your 'resultant' track – put a closed arrow-head pointing to (4) – will be your desired one. Then join (3) and (4), line (5). Now put the *parallel rules* on (5) and walk them to the *magnetic ring on the compass rose*. Read off your *heading*, say 161°M; round this to 160°M (see pages 88–9).

Finally you have no reason to suppose in this case that your errors will be greater in one direction than in another, so sketch in a circle of error round your expected position at time 1300 A.

Then you repeat exactly the same process for each subsequent hour of the passage, which will last four hours at your planning speed of 5 k. *Since this section is the nub of this book, you will do well to copy Figure 37 on to a chart, or take a similar example, and work it through.* Suppose we take successive tidal stream rates of 1·5 k, slack and 1·1 k in the opposite direction, the plot will look like Figure 38. In fact on my computations you could expect to get about 0·7 nm. from the tide on this passage, so that you would theoretically reach mark P at 1551 A. But of course this is well within your error zone so you ignore it.

Correction of planned course

So you set out from buoy O on 160°M. At 1215 A and 1230 A you get two good visual fixes (Figure 39). Clearly things are not as they should be. Your logged distances are 1·10 nm. instead of 1·25 after 15 minutes and 2·15 instead of 2·50 after 30 minutes. The wind has moderated and you are making only 4·3 k instead of 5. Also it is clear from a glance at the plot that the tidal stream, which has had

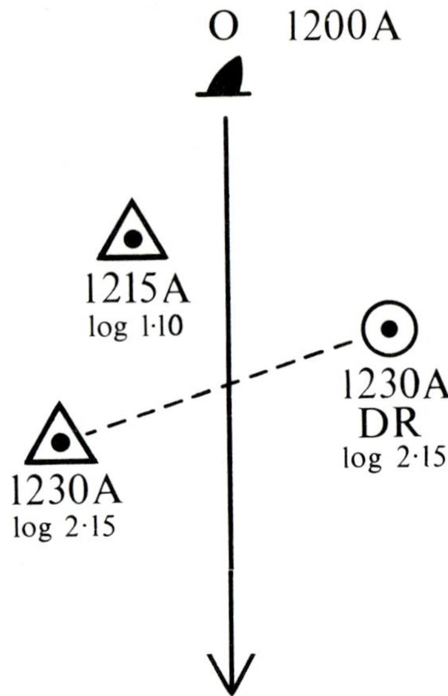

Figure 39. *Situation after 30 minutes.*

the wind over it, is running on the strong side. So you *immediately order a new heading* to stop yourself going downtide. It is very difficult to do this kind of thing cold, but I would probably change by 15° to 145°M. Certainly it pays to be bold in a case like this. Obviously the direction of the correction has to be *from your actual position towards your desired track*.

Next plot your dead reckoning position at 1230 A, using the actual log reading. Then use the procedure described in Chapter 15. Prick off the distance between the DR position and the fix; since it was taken over 30 minutes, multiply by two to get the actual tidal stream rate in knots, say 2·9 k.

Now we come back to the paradox earlier in this chapter and in the last. You made a good plan and plotted it carefully. *Your plan is now totally irrelevant; so rub it off the chart and forget it.* Buoy O is also totally irrelevant, except as a mark to fix on. By this time a quarter of an hour or so will have passed since your last fix, so take another one and plot it (Figure 40). *Draw in your new track FP. Set off drift with the corrected value, and strike an arc for your corrected speed.* You will find your heading should be 140°M. The snap correction of 15° was not quite bold enough!

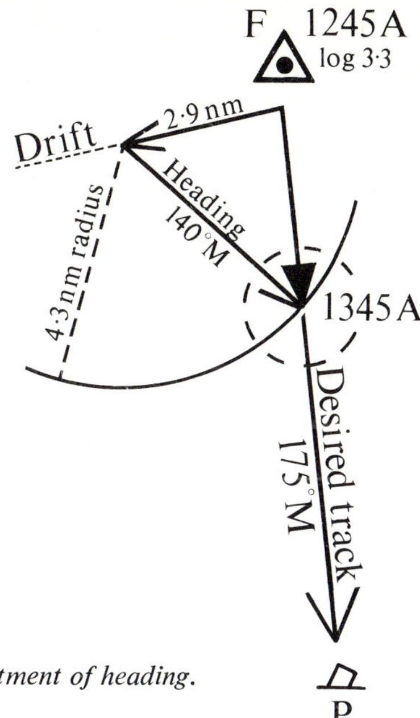

Figure 40. *Adjustment of heading.*

Having got the boat pointed in the right direction, you can go into the tidal atlas and get your corrected tidal stream rates for the next three hours. You can easily extrapolate up to 1445 A, but after that the tide should have started to turn and you will have to make some assumptions. This is where experience and above all knowledge of the waters come in. With the seat of my pants rooted firmly to the chair of my desk – and therefore pretty meaningless – I would allow for 1 to 1½ hours' overrun of the stream, take the 1400–1500 A figure (1·5 k in our basic example), extrapolate it to give, say, 2 k and apply this to the 1445–1545 A period. Similarly I should expect to have slack water for the last part of the passage.

I hope very much I have succeeded in bringing out the contrast between deliberate, meticulous planning before the passage and a determination to get better data and use them quickly once you are under way. What your course planning has really done – and this is even truer of passage and cruise planning (Chapter 20) – is to get you right into the picture and to give you a good start. *Don't let the effort you have put in beforehand make you hesitant about scrapping your plan and responding to the actual situation.*

Optimization of course

In Chapter 15 and the previous sections of this chapter I have deliberately stuck to basics and kept things simple, because an understanding of these basics is a foundation on which you can build good navigation. I have also taken a fairly extreme, though not unrealistic, example of how situations change plans. In fact your planning notes and plot will usually give you a fairly good picture of the passage. The aim of the final stage of planning is to optimize the passage. Once you have a provisional plot on the chart and all the data summarized or ready to hand, you can take another long cool look at the whole problem in terms of tide, wind and landfall.

One excellent example of this is the reverse inshore current between Cherbourg and Cap de la Hague (see page 75). Another is crossing the mouth of the Thames Estuary from Lowestoft to Ramsgate. This can be seen fairly well in the Thames Estuary Tidal Atlas in Section XIV of *Reed's* but is clearer in the Admiralty Tidal Atlas, North Sea Southern Portion (NP 251). At HWD – 5 (five hours before High Water Dover) you can see three separate flood currents starting to develop – one inshore towards Harwich, one across the mouth of the Estuary towards the North Foreland (in fact running inside the Kentish Knock) and a third 10–15 nm. further out running more southerly into the Straits of Dover. Are you going to keep inshore as far as Orford Ness and go down between Long Sand and the Kentish Knock, attempting to plug the foul tide round the North Foreland? Or are you going further out to close Ramsgate basically from the East so that you only have to *cross* the foul tide?

Again, are you going to work yourself well up to windward of the desired course – or is the wind going to change on you? If you have an offshore breeze over a high coastline, are you going to stay in the lee of the land and use the smoother water – or should you go out to get the full breeze and accept a pounding and the loss of some of the extra speed?

We discussed landfalls in Chapter 9. But are you going to aim at your destination – or at the point which you think will give you the clearest landfall? And having decided what to aim for, do you go straight for it – or 'aim off' to get up-wind or up-tide of it – and if so which?

There are no general answers to questions like these. But that does not mean that there is not a right answer, or rather a right combination of answers or compromise, for a given boat and a given passage under given conditions. The value of finding the best solution may look trivial on the chart – but it can mean the difference between saving the tide into port and taking a ten-hour battering while waiting to go in.

17
Beating

A beat is the most difficult situation with which the navigator is faced. He has lost control of heading as well as of drift. He is dependent not only on the helmsman's ability to steer a compass course, but on the watch-keeper's ability to sail the boat properly. In sum, he becomes a mere recording device. The navigator thus has a strong vested interest in working the tide to avoid beating if he can, in trying to exercise some influence on the situation and in getting off the wind as soon as he can. This is not to say that beating is not fun. In Force 4 over a fair tide on a sparkling day along a coast packed with conspicuous landmarks it can be splendid – and easy for the navigator. Beating against an over-strength tidal stream in heavy seas and driving rain has rather less appeal, at least to my taste; and accurate navigation becomes next to impossible.

Sailing close-hauled

If the navigator is not in a position to say how the boat should be sailed, he can at least complain if it is badly sailed. The trade-off between speed and consistency of heading on the one hand and angle off the wind on the other has to be right. One problem is that, having been persuaded not to pinch like he does in inland waters, an inexperienced helmsman in a stiffish boat is liable to let the head fall off about 10° without noticing it. If you sheet up too hard or pinch and stop 'slotting', the sea will knock you backwards and sideways; but 10° on a long board is a lot of mileage wasted, and luffing on a gust is just as beneficial at sea as it is round the buoys.

In pilotage conditions the boat has got to be sailed by a good helmsman just as if he were racing a dinghy on a tight circuit, using all the aids to make sure he gets the most out of her. The navigator's role is to keep track of position and warn the helmsman in good time of any dangers.

Where there is plenty of searoom and navigational techniques come into play, it is probably best to bring the boat full and by and establish a heading. Unless conditions change, you can then be reasonably certain of holding or improving on this heading. *Use the full-and-by heading for planning. Don't forget that it will be around 5° below close-hauled, so that the straddle angle between tacks will be increased by 10°* – say 85° for a typical modern cruising hull and rig. (Similarly I would suggest as yardsticks 70° for a racer and 100° for a traditional rig; but it is a question of knowing your boat.)

Once this rough datum is established, the helmsman can sail by the sails and work up to windward as best he can. He must also watch the compass, mentally average his heading and *report any changes in heading, particularly if he is forced below the 'datum' heading.*

The effects of tidal stream

We all know from experience that the effect of tide on a beating boat is very considerably greater than we should expect either from instinct or indeed from the basic drift calculation. With a fair tide, one seems to make ground almost as fast as if one were sailing straight up the desired course. With a foul tide six hours' hard beating is apt to produce negative progress. I believe this to be such an important factor in coastal cruising that it is worth exploring in depth.

First there seems to be an increasing amount of evidence (Chapters 5 and 6) that, in certain areas at least, tidal streams run much stronger with even a moderate wind over them; and even that tidal stream rates may be tending to increase generally over the years. This is a question of knowing the waters, but if the log and your feel tell you the stream is stronger than the book says, they are probably right. It would also seem that temporary increases persist after the wind that caused them has dropped, so you may be faced with a Force 6 boost to a foul tidal stream and a headwind of only Force 2–3.

Second, I am sure there is a psychological factor even with experienced helmsmen. If he is making up well past the land or in relation to a mark, the helmsman will feel he is sailing the boat well and will probably do so. If he clearly is getting nowhere, he may tend in desperation either to pinch, or to fall off in an attempt to gain at least a sensation of extra speed.

The third aspect is of course the actual drift factor. Suppose you are at position O (Figure 41), plugging tide and wind, and can make 4 k close-hauled 40° off the wind. An hour's hard work will take you exactly half a mile in the direction you want to go.

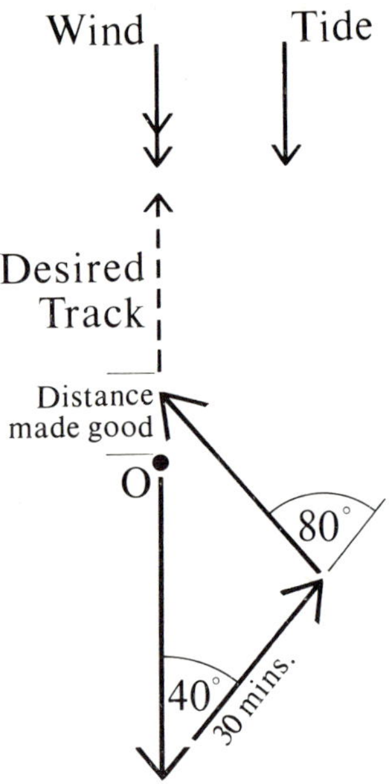

Figure 41. *Beating against the tide.*

There is however a fourth factor which is I think the one that makes things better or worse than you expect, and is not too obvious until unfortunate experiences make you think hard about it. Let us first go back to basics and consider a dinghy on a lake beating up to a mark. You will recall the effect of *apparent wind* (Figure 42*a*). Your movement towards the wind (heavy arrow) increases the wind speed in relation to your dinghy so that you go faster and can point up higher. Likewise you can luff up on a puff, as mentioned above. Now suppose you are beating downstream along a river or at sea with a fair tide. The current or tidal stream is moving your boat towards the wind at its speed of flow, *increasing* the apparent wind (Figure 42*b*); you point higher and sail faster. Conversely a foul tide

(Figure 42*c*) sets you back and *decreases* the apparent wind, so that you slow down and fall off.

In my view this 'apparent wind factor' or secondary tidal effect, which will always compound with the primary tidal effect, explains why we have all at some time or other spent five or six hours trying to beat round a headland and going steadily backwards.

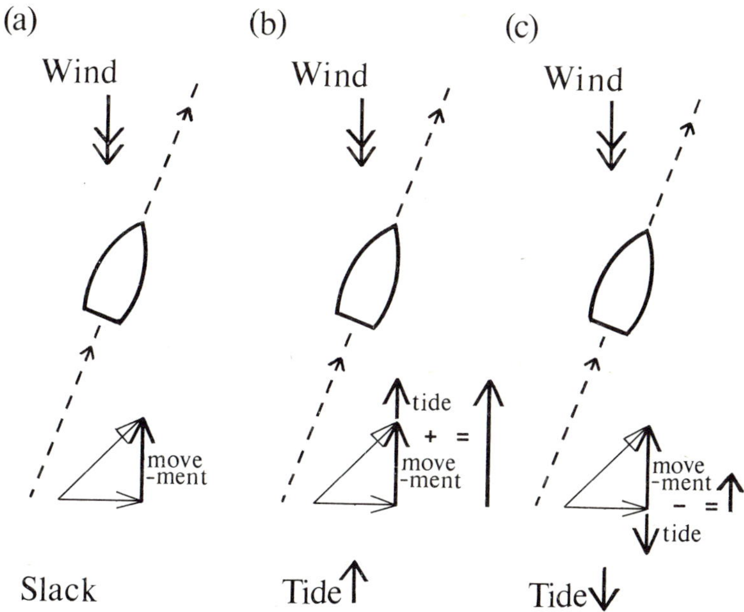

Figure 42. *Apparent wind effects: (a) no tide; (b) fair tide; (c) foul tide.*

We shall be discussing below the tactical approach to foul wind and tide but, while we are thinking in terms of primary and secondary tidal effects, it is worth considering why it is so difficult to make a change of plan pay off in this situation. Suppose (Figure 43) you are beating right inshore from position O to keep out of the worst of the tide. By the time you reach P_1 you are clearly ceasing to make past the land. So, having checked there is enough water over the bank, you decide to try and beat up over it. But in *crossing the inshore channel* you get set back, and the sea over the bank slows you down a bit, so that you finish that board at P_2. On the next tack you do a bit better, but by the time you reach P_4, near the end of the bank, you are getting a nasty head sea and more tide. Once again

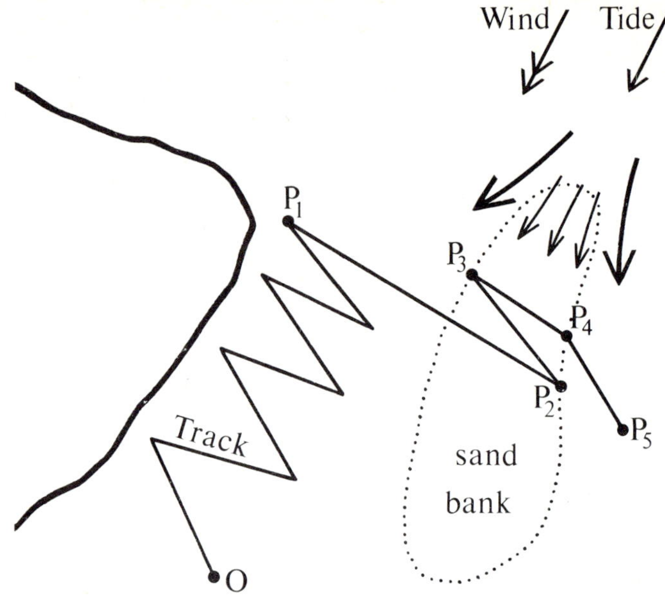

Figure 43. *Attempting to beat round a headland against a tide.*

you are clearly out of business. So you look at the tidal atlas and see fewer and less fierce arrows out to sea. This isn't just the 'greener grass principle'; the tidal stream probably *is* weaker six or seven miles out. But to get there you have to cross the inshore edge of the main channel, and back you go to P_5. I have had a number of experiences like this and am now convinced that the only answer is to choose your planned course very carefully and stick to it.

Position-finding, plotting and logging

If you are in sight of land or marks, it is best to keep a constant check on your position when beating. Unless you are approaching a danger, rough bearings off the steering compass are good enough close in. If you are working to more distant marks, you should fix every half-hour at the outside, and every quarter-hour if you are doing badly.

If you are working on corrected dead reckoning, back this up by radio fixes and allow a good safety margin over and above the calculated tidal drift. *If you are close-hauled or full and by in heavy seas under, say, reefed main and storm jib, you should allow for leeway.* Again it is best to be bold. I have found the conventional 2–3° allowance is almost always wrong, and that 5° or nothing is as good an answer as any. Above all make sure that you do not get downwind of the piece of coast you are aiming at and miss it. We have already spoken of the Cotentin Peninsula; but it is surprising how many people seem to miss even the Norfolk and Suffolk bulge coming across from Belgium or Holland.

Whatever method of position-finding you are using, *chart and log every tack*. Otherwise if you fail to make the landfall you expect you will finish up in complete confusion. If you have kept a deck-log and a dead reckoning plot going, you will have some idea where you are and can probably get a fairly accurate one by going over the plot again from your datum position and correcting it board by board.

Planning a beat

This chapter will at least have served to bring out the importance of good homework and planning when you are faced with a beat. You lose a certain amount each time you tack, but in a small boat with boards of the order of length you make at sea this is far less important than getting the best out of the conditions.

If the *tidal stream* is more or less parallel with your track, this has to be the overriding factor. If you have the tide under you, get into the channel where it runs strongest and make shortish tacks to stay there. If it is foul, do almost anything to keep out of it. As a general rule it is best to go as far inshore as you safely can. As you tack out to sea, use transits and bearings off the steering compass to check when the main tidal stream hits you. Then go about.

The tide usually runs less strongly over a bank, but make sure you stay well within the limits of the bank; poking your nose into the channels either side of it will cost you dear. Naturally you must not beat about over a bank unless you are sure there is *ample water and no risk of dangerous sea conditions* such as overfalls (see pages 81–4). A cross stream is less important until you approach the end of the passage, when you must at all costs avoid getting downwind *and* downtide of your objective. In fact if you study the cross-stream pattern carefully you may be able to choose your boards to make use of it. It is normally best to make long boards on a cross stream.

A second factor in choosing your course is *wind.* If you are well out to sea, going here or there will not make much difference except in light airs and patchy breezes. Beating does give you an odd kind of freedom of choice. Watch the clouds and get under them if you want more wind; keep clear of them if you are already wondering whether to shorten sail. Inshore, just as on inland waters, you may be able to gain quite a lot by studying the shape of the coastline and exploiting the tendency of wind to 'funnel'. For instance one would tend to stand out when off a headland and to come right in towards a valley in the hope of getting a long tack or even a fine reach. On the other hand a headwind blowing along a coast always seems to follow it round, so that it continues to head you even when you turn a corner. From both inland water and coastal sailing I have evolved a philosophy that, however many changes in direction you may seem to make, the wind for a passage is basically either fair or foul. If you start off beating, you are quite likely to stay that way.

The third factor is *sea.* Quite apart from discomfort, a short head sea can take a lot of speed off – quite enough for instance to offset the advantage of reduced tidal stream over shallow water. Thus with a foul tide you may have something of a dilemma. With a fair tide you will want to stay in the channels where the sea will usually be easiest.

I said at the beginning of the chapter that the navigator is helpless in face of a headwind. It is true there is little he can do while actually beating. But he can exercise a large measure of control in advance by diligence and cunning, in the shape of planning the boards 'tactically' and being ready to respond quickly and correctly to any change of conditions.

18
Fog

Fog is certainly the most alarming and probably the most dangerous condition the cruising yachtsman faces, particularly since it often entails a greatly increased risk of being run down. Heavy weather at night with a combination of driving rain and spray that cuts visibility right down presents much the same problems and some of its own; but at least you get much more warning of it. Dealing with fog is in many respects a matter of seamanship; we shall look purely at the navigator's contribution. As so often, the first need is a sound philosophy about it. Clearly the navigator should be geared to cope with sudden loss of visibility all the time the boat is under way. In a large, well-found boat with three trained watches and a navigator in each this can easily be done. But it is clearly not going to happen with a family crew or in many very small boats. Rather than always making a show of being prepared for fog and never in fact being so, it is better:

1. To make sure you always know where you are or can find out rather quickly.
2. To prepare properly for fog when it is forecast or the conditions make it likely.

The navigational problem is quite simply this. *By definition visual fixes will be out and pilotage nearly so*, unless you are in a channel and can creep from buoy to buoy. *Since fog is associated with calm, your log will become inaccurate, so dead reckoning will go too*, unless you motor – and this largely deprives the crew of the use of their ears.

Last visual fix

If you see features or lights vanishing and reappearing, or if you see a fog bank rolling in, *your immediate action must be to get a visual fix.* If you are too late, your previous visual fix becomes a key piece of information.

Use of radio aids

Much will depend on whether you have set up your DF radio in advance. Chapter 13 suggests that you should list your radio beacons in advance just as you do lights (see page 66), set up your DF radio and select the most suitable stations early in the passage while you can double check the radio against a visual fix. You should also have rechecked the radio DF situation during the passage as you moved from one area to another. If you have done all this, you should be able to go over to working on DF radio quickly and effectively. Otherwise it is probably worth closing a buoy if you safely can and taking a radio fix a cable or so off it to confirm that you are getting a correct position.

The problem is, however, that radio fixes taken in small boats are not as a rule all that accurate; a lot of errors are involved and some of them are quite large. It will therefore often help to bring in a local radio beacon that you would not normally use, such as the one at Cherbourg, or to try and take a bearing on an aviation beacon if there is one in the right place and within your set's frequency range. The *homing technique* described on pages 138–9 is useful in fog, *provided you are on a safe approach line.* Some people home on a beacon in desperation from wherever they may be – or think they are – and this can be very dangerous indeed.

Sound signals

Once again if you have followed the advice in Chapter 4 and have included sound signals in your list of lights, you will have no problem. Otherwise you must make a list as soon as there is any likelihood of fog. In any case it is worth rechecking your list and seeing if there are any additional marks with sound signals that might be useful in your actual situation. As with lights (pages 52–4), the period of a sound signal is its complete cycle, not the silent interval.

Soundings and tidal information

One of the odder human characteristics is the ability to surpass one's form and physical limitations when it matters. Fog deprives you of your most accurate methods of finding your way, so you have got somehow to beat the error systems of the less accurate ones. Precise tidal information becomes essential where rough estimates would serve if you could see. On the one hand, if you are becalmed in a fog you need to know exactly what the tidal stream is going to do to you. On the other you need a *precise depth above chart datum.*

You will recall from Chapter 13 that soundings are a valuable back-up to the DF radio. Generally you need this double check when you are well out to sea with so much water under you that the height of the tide is neither here nor there – you are looking say for the difference between 30 m and 60 m. In fog, when you are close inshore and desperately need the DF radio to be right, you must be able to correct for tide height if you are to use relatively shallow soundings with small differences as a position check.

There are really two things you need to do. One is to rework or recheck the tidal information from the almanac, tidal atlas and chart (Chapters 5 and 6). The second is to refine this data with measurements from your plot, as described on pages 130 and 152–3.

Possible courses of action

Whether to drop anchor or motor when caught in a fog are seamanship decisions. But if you decide to keep going you have four basic options. One is to *stand off*, but fog is the one case in which the rule, 'If in doubt, stand out', needs to be taken with a pinch of salt. On the one hand you have to steer clear of dangers or shallow water; on the other – and above all – *you have got to minimize the risk of being run down.* It is therefore best to find a safe-looking area outside buoyed channels or shipping lanes, and preferably with plenty of water for you but too little for commercial shipping.

The second is to *enter harbour*. This is undeniably the most attractive course, but in my view rather seldom a sound one. If the port is large enough to have a deep, wide, clearly marked channel and all the aids you need to get in, it will probably have shipping coming in and out of it and the risk of being run down will be unacceptably high.

The third option is to *work your way from buoy to buoy*, with the aid of the compass if needs be, staying just clear of the main channel if it is channel markers you are using. Provided that the risk of being run down is not excessive, this is often the best thing to do. It does not matter if you have to sail to and fro or round in circles. If you move from mark to mark you have a pretty accurate idea of your position; and if you are underway you can take immediate avoiding action if needs be.

The three possibilities above share the assumption that you were in a safe, sensible and known position when visibility closed down. Very often however fog seems to come down when you are badly out of position so that you have a navigational problem anyway. With fog, a fluky wind, a strong tide running and doubt about your position, you really do have to get the seat of your pants working. Clearly you stand out, even if you have to motor. On the other hand, if you just head out to sea and the fog stays down you are liable to get well and truly lost unless your DF radio is behaving itself unusually well. It is therefore best if possible to head for a seaward mark with a sound signal. I must admit to having in mind here the wreck buoy (old system) in the middle of the Seine Bay, which has twice got me out of trouble in fog. Dead reckoning with corrections for tide can do very well for you if you take enough trouble and are prepared to mess the helmsman about with frequent minor adjustments of heading or calls for a heading if he is on the wind.

A final key point is that someone should double check often, if not continuously, that the helmsman is holding the heading ordered and not the reciprocal or something else. Fog is very confusing for helmsmen, too, and it is not easy to steer a compass course when you have nothing to look at but the compass, and bare steerage way on.

19

Entrances

Entering a port or estuary for the first time is probably the greatest challenge that faces the navigator of a typical cruising yacht. Equally, of course, it demands high standards of seamanship. Under bad conditions even familiar ports can be tricky. It is difficult to recall an entrance which does not present some kind of problem, the common element being lack of searoom; this means that mistakes must be avoided rather than made and then corrected. Leaving harbour requires just as much care – a fact that is often forgotten, sometimes with serious consequences.

Types of entrance and their problems

Most *major ports* have a high intensity of commercial traffic, some of it large enough virtually to fill the whole channel and much of it operating to very tight schedules. This means you have got to plan:

1. Where you are going to go if you have to clear the approach channel or even double back in front of a bottleneck.
2. Where you are going to moor or anchor temporarily if you have to wait for a lock or a berth.
3. If possible, whether you can safely keep clear of the shipping channel for all or part of the way in.

Minor ports and fishing ports often have badly marked channels which may only be usable at certain states of the tide. There may be very little room to manoeuvre or berth inside, and few if any deep-water berths. Some form of local knowledge or advice is usually indispensable.

With *estuaries, river mouths and some minor ports* the problem – or at least the danger – lies outside the entrance rather than within it. The outflow of a river tends to produce a narrow channel with a bar on one side and a spit on the other (Figure 44). There may also be wide sand or mud banks which will lead to strong local cross sets while the tide is flooding them. You must *always go in on the flood* –

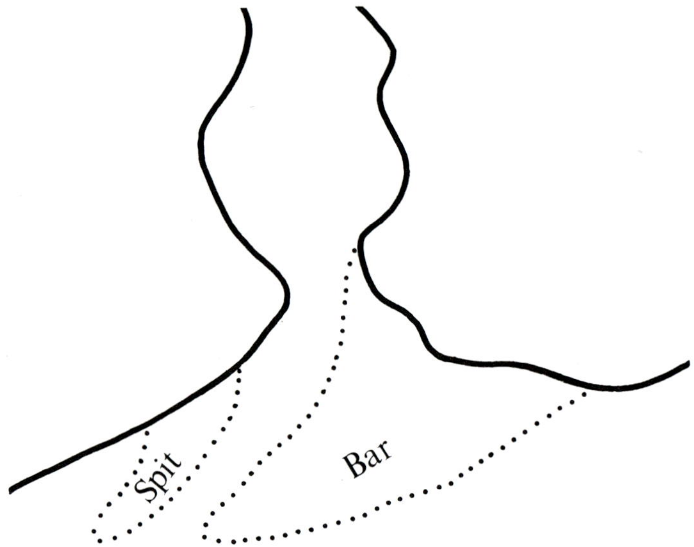

Figure 44. *A typical bar and spit river mouth.*

more of this later – and some entrances such as the River Ore/Alde in Suffolk are regarded as so dangerous that one is advised to leave on the flood as well. These kinds of entrance should *never be attempted if there is a heavy sea running*, and choppy areas may be dangerous even when the general sea state is moderate (Valentia in Eire is a good example of this). Going aground on a *shingle bar* carries a very high risk of severely damaging or losing the boat; with *sand bars* the immediate danger is somewhat less but you will at best be in for a very unpleasant time. Another problem is that, while commercial and fishing ports almost always have some lights, even major yachting centres often have completely unlit approaches. Examples of this are the River Blackwater (West Mersea) and even the Crouch, where the last 15 miles in have no navigational lights.

Choice of day or night entrance

In choosing between daylight and darkness you really need to consider landfall (Chapter 9) and entrance together. If possible avoid the two hours or so astride dawn; this is the time when mist or sea fog is most probable and when the human biological cycle is at its lowest, thus increasing the risk of mistakes. Broadly speaking major and medium commercial ports on coasts with good navigational lights and no other large towns are best entered at night. Large towns mask navigational lights, and ill-lit coasts, minor ports and estuaries are best approached by day, at least until you know them very well. It is also to some extent a matter of personal preference. Going into a major port for the first time, I would generally choose to enter by night and leave by day (so as to get a good look at it for next time); but if there was very heavy traffic – Harwich/Felixstowe for instance – I would go in by day.

Information and local advice

Making an entrance for the first time is the situation that really brings home all that was said in the early chapters of this book about compiling information that is reliable, precise, double checked and *above all up-to-date*. A *large-scale chart* or harbour plan is very useful the first time, although on subsequent occasions you will probably go in and out off the medium-scale approach chart. *Photographs* such as the Adlard Coles series and other 'unofficial' pilots give are invaluable; however good you are at building up a mental picture from a chart, charts do not always give as much ground detail as you need to do this. You must make yourself completely familiar with all marks, studying their physical characteristics as well as their lights and/or sound signals so that you can recognize them quickly. As stressed in Chapter 4, making a list is a good way of doing this as well as being useful for reference. The same goes for port entry signals and associated sailing directions (*Reed's* Sections X and XI).

Some channels can shift every few days under certain conditions of wind and tide. For minor ports it is always worth *ringing up the harbour-master* to get a last-minute briefing as well as to book a berth or mooring. *Reed's* lists harbour-masters' telephone numbers at the beginning of Section X. Many people are hesitant about doing this, but I have never received anything but the greatest courtesy and helpfulness. The next best contact is the *secretary of the local sailing club*, if you can discover its name; but remember that some estuary clubs concentrate entirely on dinghy sailing. If there is no harbour-master or suitable yacht club, the nearest *Coastguard* station or the local *police* will usually be able to tell you who to get in touch with. This may be a fisherman; they often club together to buoy minor channels for their own use. In one instance I know (Blakeney) the contact is the warden of the nature reserve. Time and telephone charges spent in getting such information are well worthwhile. Obviously this is not going to be easy in foreign waters; even if you or one of your crew speak the language, telephone costs are high and it is not always easy to get through. When going foreign it is best to make for a relatively large port first. Yacht clubs are usually only too pleased to help foreign visitors, and the harbour-master or Coastguard station (or the equivalent) will usually get the information for you.

In many cases however even last-minute local information is not enough and a pilot is the only safe solution. It is much less easy than it used to be to arrange for a pilot (usually a local fisherman) in minor ports and estuaries, although where feasible it often costs surprisingly little and is certainly worth doing. An alternative is to anchor off or beat about in safe water at low tide and follow a fishing boat or other local boat in. Don't follow another yacht, unless you are sure he knows the waters! Local knowledge, information and assistance is tremendously important but it is a complement to, not a substitute for, good basic data and diligent homework.

Sailing in confined waters, which may have strong tides running and be partly or fully exposed to wind and sea, calls for a good look-out and a very quick response. Having compiled your information and made your plan, *brief the whole crew thoroughly* on dangers, marks, traffic hazards and recognition features so that they can all contribute. This will also minimize the 'Oh look, whatever's that?' type of question at moments when you may have your hands full. Night entrances in particular call for good intercommunication (see pages 63–4).

Use of marks and choice of course

In making an approach and entrance, choice of course becomes inseparable from the boat's capabilities and more particularly its vices. Weatherliness is one critical factor; in many narrow channels and entrances beating is either impossible or asking for trouble. Equally relevant are any characteristics of the rigging – or the crew! – that make for slow sail-handling, especially lowering. Restriction of visibility between lowering and furling the mainsail may be critical. Handling under power is even more important, particularly in confined and crowded waters with a strong tide; if your boat has vices in turning tightly through the wind under power (high freeboard forward) or going astern (screw rotation effect), these must be recognized and taken into account. *Speed* is another factor; clearly you must not carry too much sail, especially large genoas which slow down manoeuvre; and you must reduce speed sufficiently to give adequate observation and reaction time. On the other hand, if you have too little way on you may get set all over the place by the tide, or even spun by an eddy, and you may not be able to take avoiding action quickly enough.

On the approach, you must make a major effort to *pick up the leading marks or lights early*, get on to bearing and hold on it if you can. If you have to beat, make short boards straddling the approach line evenly – if of course dangers and depth allow this. Where you have more searoom, and as you close and have to take account of traffic and channel or danger markers, you should if possible choose a course that you will be able to hold under sail, with due allowance for the lee of tall objects, funnelling, and other tricks of the wind. Leave yourself *as much room as possible to leeward and downtide*, having checked how far outside the channel and/or below your chosen course you have good water.

Another important factor in choosing your course will often be *field of view*. In a twisting or dog-leg channel with high or built-up banks you should steer to 'open' the channel as far ahead of you as possible. This is important both for acquiring the next marks and of course for seeing shipping or other obstructions in time to react comfortably. When you are virtually blind – the main entrance and the turn between outer and inner ports at Cherbourg are good examples of this – you must be ready to react instantly.

Often the most important single factor in planning an entrance will be the *state of the tide*. It is clearly best to go in on the flood, even if safety does not dictate this. In some cases you will need two or three hours of flood under you to have enough water to enter at all or at least to have any room for manoeuvre. But generally speaking it is both safest and most comfortable to start the entrance as early on the flood as you can. Dangers are visible, the major cross set will probably not have begun, and with luck there may not yet be enough water for commercial shipping to move freely. As against this entering high tide may enable you to keep completely clear of the main channel and to beat freely if you need to. You must judge each case on its merits. One important aspect of timing, however, is restrictions caused by low bridges, locks or basin gates. By entering at low water, you may be able to get under a bridge without lowering your mast or by lowering it very slightly; at high water you may have to lower it completely and even unstep it. *Most sea locks and basin gates operate only for an hour or so either side of high water*; *Reed's* gives the exact timings (Sections X and XI). It is pleasant enough to anchor or tie up for an hour or two and sort yourself out before the lock gate or basin opens, but extremely trying and probably dangerous to have to wait nine or ten hours, some of it on a falling tide.

Planning an entrance

Once you head into the approach channel you are psychologically committed to making the entrance; tide and other factors may commit you physically. Thus you need to envisage and plan the entrance as a whole from the moment you pick up the leading lights or close the outer channel markers until you are alongside, on a mooring or at anchor.

Other things being equal, it is best to work backwards from your intended berth, or the lock or basin gate, and the time you want to arrive there – as we shall see in the next chapter one does just this in planning a passage. There may however be other *critical sections or features of the approach and entrance* on which you must base your plan. These may be such things as depth; dangerous sea conditions at certain states of the tide (notably over bars); traffic; visibility problems from looking into a setting sun; need for room to lower sail safely; or the fact that between high quays vision at low tide is limited and you cannot see, for example, the Customs House, or exactly where you are in relation to it.

By looking at the problem as a whole, you can pick out the critical point, decide the timing that you want to pass it in terms of tide and light and work out how much difference either side of your chosen time you can accept. If this critical point is not your final berth or mooring, you must next check that the latter does not impose a secondary limitation – for instance that if you cross the bar with 3 m of water under you, you can still reach the lock before it closes. In this way you arrive at a complete timed plan and can say when you must arrive at the seaward mark or when and where you must be to pick up the leading marks. This provides the basis for your passage plan.

20

Passage Preparation and Planning

Planning is something of a dirty word nowadays; at best it marches ill with romantic notions of messing about in boats and the timelessness of cruising under sail. I am sure many people feel – as I do – a real philosophical conflict here, a temptation to push off regardless into the blue. Certainly you can make a one-tide passage down a coast you know well or cruise about in a familiar estuary without too much thought in advance – although even these activities can end in tears. But if you put out into major shipping lanes, sail out of sight of land or enter strange ports, you will put the lives of your crew and of members of the rescue services at avoidable risk, and maybe damage or lose your boat, unless you make a sensible plan. And it is planning and the motor – neither of them particularly attractive in itself – that put sailing into the time-frame of modern life. In fact, planning a cruise in advance is great fun; together with the planning of individual passages, it will add greatly to the crew's pleasure and offer a reasonable chance of getting them home refreshed and above all punctually.

The purpose of planning a passage is to get the best out of the boat, the conditions and the crew's time – and to exercise the greatest possible degree of control over the situation. Like most other kinds of plan, your carefully worked-out passage may never come to fruition; but in studying it you will have briefed yourself to deal with the situation that actually arises.

Documentation

The first task is to assemble all the data sources you need and make sure they are up to date (Chapter 1). In particular check charts (including emergency coverage), almanac and tidal atlas(es). Also make sure you have the latest edition of any sailing directions, official and otherwise. Do this well in advance, in case there is any problem about obtaining the new documentation. It is maddening to have to change your plans because you have not got a chart you know you will need; or (as nearly happened to me very recently) to have to postpone a cruise because you have forgotten to get a new *Reed's Nautical Almanac* and all the local shops have sold out. You need incidentally to budget for documentation both at the beginning of the season and before each cruise.

Having assembled the documents, do as much of the homework on them as you can in advance. Make lists of key marks and lights (see page 66), mark up tidal atlases (see pages 74–5), and read yourself in to the whole cruise without going into too much detail.

Before each passage double check the charts you will need, clean them if necessary and make sure that the rest of the documentation is under your hand and in usable condition.

Chartroom and instruments

Make sure you have all the stationery you need, including weather forecast pads and a suitable exercise book or notebook as a working log. Check over all the instruments – compass (pages 30–5 and Chapter 12), DF radio (pages 35–6 and Chapter 13), log (pages 36–9 and Chapter 14) and echo-sounder (pages 39–40) – and of course two-way RT and radar if you have these. In particular check that your compass light and any other illumination needed to navigate at night are working, not forgetting the chart light, map-reading torch and other torches – and all spare bulbs and batteries. Check your plotting instruments for damage and clean them; in particular make doubly sure you have parallel rules and dividers with you. (Not long ago I was in a crew of eight, including three qualified skippers, which nearly managed to sail without parallel rules!) It is worth making a physical check on all this before each passage, even if you are 'sure' that all is well. Defects and losses seem to go in runs, and it does not take many to make you virtually unable to navigate effectively.

Making the passage plan

In the event one usually makes a cruise plan first, then looks at the passages in it and then recycles the cruise plan, so that the final passage plans are the last thing to be done. But I think it will be helpful to consider a single passage first, drawing together the various skills and procedures I have set out in this book. Much depends on the nature and length of the passage and on the conditions – and to some extent on the individual navigator. Let me therefore explain the sequence I normally follow and some of the thinking behind it.

First take a general look at the whole problem. Find the *total distance* with a large-scale chart and dividers, pricking it off leg by leg. Take this from the point at which you finally clear harbour and stream your log to the outer mark of your destination. Make adequate allowance for the distance you will have to cover standing out to sea and back and keeping a safe distance off lee shores (5 nm. is a good yardstick) and round headlands. If there is a tide-race round a headland, you may have to go several miles out to avoid its danger zone. Then look at the weather forecast and plump for a *planning speed*; divide this by *three* for any leg you may have to beat. This will give you a realistic, if somewhat depressing idea of *how long the passage is going to take*. Unless I know the ports concerned, I normally allow *three hours each for clearing and entering* – that is from when you slip to when you set course and from when you start worrying about lining up for the entrance until you are berthed. This seldom proves pessimistic; even the shortest and simplest of entrances is apt to take about an hour in all. And this is a significant point because you have got to weigh up the pros of intermediate ports of call against the time and effort involved in getting in and out. To conclude this first stage, take a look at any *dangers or restrictions on the way* and note these; for instance you may prefer to cross the Straits of Dover shipping lanes in daylight or to avoid closing Weymouth through the worst of the Portland Race ebb. Such dangers are a key factor that may lead you to change your destination or to call – or not to call – at an intermediate port.

After satisfying yourself with this rough check, start with the *entrance*, working from the berth or critical point outwards and above all checking lock timings (see pages 180–1). This will give you a series of *times and tide states off your destination*. Then look at the *landfall problem* (Chapter 9). Consider landfall and entrance together and *choose between day and night* (see pages 106 and 177). Before going firm, check back over restrictions en route in case they modify this choice. If you decide on a landfall off the direct line of approach to your destination, allow for sailing from landfall to entrance. You will then have a *firm time and tide state for your expected landfall.*

Using the passage time figure from your rough check, you can then decide *which tide you must leave on.* Unless there is some reason to the contrary, *take the fair tidal stream first* (Chapter 6) to get some mileage in your belly. This gives you a *time to set course.* Then make your plan for clearing harbour (Chapters 5, 8 and (in reverse) 19). This will give you a *time to slip.*

Starting with the time at which you set course and stream your log, work right through the passage (Chapter 16), at this stage not hourly but tide by tide, six-hourly that is, except where you have to make short legs to round headlands or clear dangers. This will give you a more accurate idea of distance and, much more important, of the expected point of sailing on each leg and the amount of help or hindrance you will get from the tide. From this you can work out a *time for each leg* and thence a *passage time*, to which you must add your clearing and entrance times.

If possible get a second person to check through all your workings, going right back to source. Once these are confirmed, all you have to do is to write up your final list of marks and lights (see page 66) and radio beacons (see pages 134–5), and your sailing notes.

Time margins

The first thing that needs saying about time margins in passage planning is: 'Don't cheat yourself or let others pressure you into cheating.' Over-ambitious planning may well mean you have to wait ten hours or so outside your destination. The crew will be tired, morale will sag and if conditions are at all rough a dangerous situation may develop. If you can get in at any time, if necessary by plugging the ebb with the engine, fair enough. But if there is a restriction of tide state or of locking through, *allow a complete extra tide (twelve hours) in your planning.* If you save the earlier tide, everyone will be delighted; if not – well, you are still on schedule.

As for clearing and entering, I have stressed above the need to allow ample time without going to absurd lengths. You can always kill time but you cannot bring it back to life. A casual underestimate of an hour in the time you need to clear your home port can cost you twelve hours or, if your destination port is unlit, twenty-four hours at the far end.

Time margins for the main passage are very difficult to consider in cold blood. Only the person who plans the course knows what hidden reserves he has built into his plan. On the one hand it would be foolish not to allow some margin on a long passage when arrival time is critical. On the other, if you over-allow, you will cripple the whole cruise plan to no good purpose. I will stick my neck out for the last time and say what I do. First, in the rough check, I use the motorist's rule of adding 10 per cent to the distance and take a deliberately conservative estimate of speed. This gives an extended duration and ensures – always subject to changes of weather – that my detailed entrance and clearance planning is realistic.

Then, in laying off my planned course in detail, I allow a slight margin for rounding marks, clearing dangers and so on. This is really a safeguard against all the errors compounding the wrong way. In interpolating in tidal stream rates, I use figures two days nearer neaps than the actual day for fair tides and two days nearer springs for foul – unless of course I have enough information to make a reasonable prediction of abnormal variations (see page 68). Once under way, I go all out to gain a tide on my plan by refining it. I apologize for this subjective exposé, but I can think of nothing clearer-cut or more general that might not be misleading.

Contingency and emergency plans

Having made your main plan, you then need to look at a heavy-weather plan or plans. Basically you need to consider a gale from any of the four quadrants and *its effect on sea state*; the latter is particularly important off exposed coasts such as those facing the North Sea or the Atlantic, when sea may be more dangerous than the wind itself and is certainly going to persist much longer. Which of the four quadrants you devote most attention to will depend on:

1. The main direction of your course.
2. The lie of the land on either side of it.
3. The meteorological trends in your area.
4. The general weather situation at the time.

You have also to consider both being able to maintain a chosen course off the wind under shortened sail and having to run under bare poles with streamed warps or to come hull-to.

The other contingencies you have to consider are damage to the boat and illness or injury – or of course the loss of a key crew member.

The most useful thing to do is probably to examine your course leg by leg, *list the refuge ports* to either side of it and above all *check that you have the necessary chart cover and sailing directions* to get into them under difficult conditions. In other words, if you have a gale warning or bad weather forecast to which you must respond, you should know straight away where you are going to make for.

Cruise planning

Planning a whole cruise, as opposed to a single passage, is very much a function of the performance and facilities of the boat and even more of the stamina and tastes of the crew. From the navigational point of view, one can only comment on limitations of space and time. Unless your boat and crew are in every sense of the words fit and equipped to ride out a severe gale in the open sea – as many yachts over 9–10 m and rather fewer crews are – you should *never be more than eight hours' running or motoring at say 5 k from an all-weather port of refuge – maybe 50 nm. at the absolute outside*. This is the yardstick I use for my present boat with a small, not fully trained crew; and I suspect it to have fairly wide application.

In timing a cruise you have the threefold pressure of safety, crew stamina and getting back on time. In northern European waters, except the Baltic, I start by writing off one day in seven, even in the season of the Easterlies. I then plan the first passage or two so that I have a sporting chance of making up twelve and maybe twenty-four hours without undue pressure on the crew. With only one qualified watch, I would regard eighteen hours of passage, excluding clearing and entering, as the normal limit, with twenty-four hours as the extreme. This assumes of course that there will be periods during which the qualified individual can at least go below. With two watches, I would limit passage time to forty-eight hours with an exceptional seventy-two hours. With three watches there is no limit in terms of human resources.

On the same theme, I would think in terms of not more than one night running out of port with one watch and two nights with two watches. Whether or not I was gale-bound for my 'reserve' day, I would take one day a week completely ashore. So much depends on conditions; with Force 3/4 and Sea State 1, staying at sea is far less effort than putting into and out of harbour. This cautious approach will I know seem ridiculous to many who read this book; but I am thinking mainly of small crews, particularly of family crews, where both skills and stamina are limited.

In the second half of this book I have written much about planning and prediction, because these are fun in themselves and add greatly to the safety and enjoyment of cruising. I should like to close by reminding the reader of the two paradoxes I stated in Chapters 15 and 16:

1. You cannot navigate without a datum position; but once you have a new datum, all before it is irrelevant.
2. You must make a careful and precise plan for each passage and each leg of it; but you must be ready to tear this up the moment you get to sea and acquire new firm data.

In like vein, a very experienced language teacher once described grammar to me as 'like a pair of crutches to an injured man – once you are really fit, you can discard them.' The same is true of this book. I wish its readers happy sailing and hope they may rapidly educate the seat of their pants to the point where they can consign the book to the attic or the waves.

Appendix 1

Navigator's Checklists

At the start of season/before each cruise/on take-over of boat

Documentation

Chart cover – full, emergency. Up-to-date?
Relevant *Notices to Mariners.*
Sailing directions – official, unofficial, local. Amendments/supplements?
Admiralty List of Lights (or local equivalent). Amendments?
Reed's Nautical Almanac – Current? Updating supplement?
Tidal atlas(es).
Admiralty Chart 5011 (booklet form) – up-to-date?
Yachtsman's Dictionary (see Bibliography).

Chart folios.
Charts correctly arranged and numbered.
Map-case (see pages 21–2).

Instruments

Barometer – functioning?

Clock(s) – wound and set.
Portable radio – AM/FM including long wave.
DF radio – functioning?
RT set – functioning? Antenna OK?
Steering compass – cockpit mounting? Light?
Hand-bearing compass – light?
Emergency compass.

Log/speedometer:
  Patent – line, sinker, spinner, spares, oil.
  Electromagnetic – functioning? Spare transducer? Tools for access to, and stripping of transducer?
Echo-sounder – functioning?
Leadline.
Binoculars – check for double-imaging and fungus.
Radar – functioning?

Protractor.
Parallel rules.
Dividers – large and small.
Compasses.
Map-reading torch.
Chart light.
Pocket calculator.
Pencil sharpener.

Working and spare batteries? Spare bulbs?

Stationery

Weather forecast pad.
Pad for rough working.
Pad/exercise book for deck-log.
Log-book.
Hard and soft pencils.
Hard and soft erasers.
Ballpoints.

Before each passage

Recheck cover – charts, sailing directions, amendments, etc.
Charts clean.
Working charts handy.
Harbour plan in map-case.
Recheck *all* instruments and lights.
Spare bulbs/batteries replaced if used?
Log spares?
Weather forecasts – clip (with existing charts/notes) and pad.
Deck-log ready.
Check stationery stocks.

Appendix 2

Notes on Some Foreign Charts and Sailing Directions

Most yachtsmen will normally prefer to use charts and navigational documentation of their own country, and there are many advantages in doing so. On the other hand they may want to penetrate waters for which large-scale cover is only available from local sources; or to expand or intensify their chart cover while in a foreign port.

The key international index to documentation is the *Yearbook of the International Hydrographic Organization*; this agency is based in Monte Carlo, Monaco, and its Yearbook (bilingual, French and English) gives the details of organizations in all member countries.

In principle and increasingly in practice, greatly helped by the introduction of the IALA 'A' Buoyage system, symbols used on charts are international. *The key point to check is the unit used for soundings – fathoms, metres or feet.* For Anglo-Saxon sailors used to fathoms, a confusion here can be expensive! If one is sailing in marginal waters, as many cruising yachtsmen would wish to do, a check must be made on the *chart datum* used (see table on page 69). As far as wording is concerned, Barbara Webb's *Yachtsman's Eight-Language Dictionary*, mentioned in Chapter 1, is a great help.

Many countries publish their verbal documentation bilingually in their own language and English. Where the use of a different alphabet or an ideographic language makes even charts totally unintelligible, it will often be possible to use charts of a neighbouring country with a readable alphabet.

The table below lists the organizations of selected countries together with the references of their chart/document catalogues and their UK agencies if any.

Country	*Organization*	*Title/ref. of catalogue*	*Language*	*UK agent*
Argentine	Servicio de Hidrografía Naval Avenida Montes de Oca 212 Buenos Aires	H.223	Spanish	
Australia	Royal Australian Navy Hydrographic Service Garden Island New South Wales 2000	5020a (North) 5020b (South)	English	Hydrographic Department Ministry of Defence Taunton
Belgium	Ministerie van Openbare Werken Bestuur der Waterwegen Residentie De Mast E. Feysplein, B–8400 Oostende	(not known)	French/ Flemish	
Brazil	Diretoria de Hidrografia e Navegação Ministério da Marinha Rio de Janeiro	DN63–8 (Supplements have small letter suffix, e.g. DN63–8a)	Portuguese	
Canada	Canadian Hydrographic Service IB 615 Booth Street Ottawa, Ontario K1A OH3	1. Great Lakes, etc. 6. Northwest 11. Hudson Bay, etc. 13. Southern B. Col. 14. Northern B. Col. 15. Arctic (?) Atlantic		Kelvin Hughes, Glasgow and London

Chile	Instituto Hidrográfico de la Armada Casilla 324 Valparaiso	IHA Pub. 3000	Spanish	
Denmark	Farvandsdirektoratet Nautisk Afdeling Esplanaden 19 DK–1263 Copenhagen	INDEKS I Denmark INDEKS II Greenland	Danish/ English	Kelvin Hughes, Glasgow Olsens, Grimsby Dubois-Phillips & McCallum, Liverpool Capt. Watts, London
Finland	Merenkulkuhallitus Merikarttaosasto Vuorimiehenkatu 1 00 140 Helsinki 14	'Catalogue of Finnish Charts' (plus year of pub.)	English Finnish Swedish	
France	Service Hydrographique et Océanographique de la Marine 3, Avenue Octave Gréard F–75200 Paris-Naval	Fascicule 4 A – Europe B – Africa and East C – Americas	French	
Germany (GDR)	Seehydrographischer Dienst de DDR Rostock	8800	German	
Germany (FRG)	Deutsches Hydrographisches Institut Bernhard-Nocht-Strasse 78 Postfach 220 D–2000 Hamburg 4	2452	German	J. D. Potter, London

Country	*Organization*	*Title/ref. of catalogue*	*Language*	*UK agent*
Iceland	Sjómaelingar Íslands Seljavegi 32 PO Box 7094 Reykjavik	'Sjókort' 'Charts'	Icelandic/ English	
Italy	Istituto Idrografico della Marina Passo Osservatorio 4 I–16100 Genova	F.C. 1051	Italian	
Japan	Kaijōhoan-Chō Suiro-Bu No. 3–1, 5-Chōme, Tsukiji, Chūo-Ku, Tokyo 104	Pub. No. 900	Japanese (parts in English)	
Netherlands	Afdeling Hydrografie van het Ministerie van Defensie (Marine) 171, Badhuisweg 's-Gravenhage	'Catalogue of Charts' (plus year of pub.)	Dutch/ English	
New Zealand	Hydrographic Office Royal New Zealand Navy PO Box 33341 Takapuna Auckland 9	N.Z. 200	English	Dubois-Phillips & McCallum, Liverpool Kelvin Hughes, London
Norway	Norges Sjøkartverk Klubbgt. 1 Stavanger	OVERSIKT (plus year of pub.)	Norwegian	Olsens, Grimsby Edward Stanford, London

Peru	Dirección de Hidrografía y Navegación de la Marina Sáenz Peña Cuactra 5ta. La Punta	HIDRONAV-3300	Spanish	
Spain	Instituto Hidrográfico de la Marina Tolosa Latour N° 1 Cadiz	Catálogo de Cartas Nauticas, etc.	Spanish	
Sweden	Sjökarteavdelningen Sjöfartsverket, Fack S–60101 Norrköping	'Swedish Charts and Nautical Publications'	Swedish/ English	Capt. Watts, London John Lilley & Gillie, North Shields
Turkey	Seyir Hidrografi ve Osinografi Dairesi Baskanliğu Çubuklu, Istanbul	DS 84–S/E	Turkish	
Uruguay	Servicio de Oceanografía e Hidrografia de la Armada Capurro 980 Casilla de Correo 1380 Montevideo	Catálogo de Cartas y Publicaciónes	Spanish	
USA	Distribution Division, C44 National Ocean Survey Riverdale Maryland 20840	Nautical Chart Catalogs 1 – Atlantic and Gulf Coasts 2 – Pacific Coast 3 – Alaska	English	Capt. Watts, London John Lilley & Gillie, North Shields (See Bibliography)

Country	*Organization*	*Title/ref. of catalogue*	*Language*	*UK agent*
USSR	Glavnoe Oupravlenie Navigatsii i Okeanografii Ministerstva Oborony 8, 11 liniya, B–34 Leningrad 199034	7007	Russian	
Yugoslavia	Hidrografski Institut Jugoslavenske Ratne Mornarice Split	HI–N–18	Serbo- Croat	

Bibliography

Further and related reading

Blewitt, Mary, *Navigation for Yachtsmen* (Stanford Maritime).
Blewitt, Mary, *Celestial Navigation for Yachtsmen* (Stanford Maritime).
Sex, Tim, *Coastwise Cruising* (Nautical Publishing Co.).

References

Reed's Nautical Almanac (*Reed's*).
Webb, Barbara, *Yachtsman's Eight-Language Dictionary* (Adlard Coles).

Official charts and documentation

BRITISH: See catalogues of Hydrographer of the Navy Publications (NP 131 world-wide, NP 91 home edition) for:
- Admiralty charts
- Admiralty pilots
- Admiralty lists of lights
- Admiralty tidal atlases

Notices to Mariners (free if collected, or for cost of postage)

Note. All the above are available from Admiralty chart agents, usually chandlers. Your local harbour-master or chief pilot can give you the nearest address.

FOREIGN: See Appendix 2.

Unofficial sailing directions and navigation books

Brandon, Robin. *South Biscay Pilot*. 2nd ed. Adlard Coles, 1977.

——. *South France Pilot*, 6 vols. Imray, 1976.

Bristol Channel Yachting Conference Handbook.

Campbell, Capt. F. S. *Stanford's Harbour Guide: North Foreland to the Needles*. Stanford Maritime, 1975.

——. *Stanford's Harbour Guide: River Medway and the Swale.* Stanford Maritime, 1975.

——. *Stanford's Harbour Guide to the West Coast of Scotland.* Stanford Maritime, 1973.

Clyde Cruising Club. *Sailing Directions and Achorages*. 3 vols. (West Coast of Scotland; North and North East Coasts of Scotland; Orkneys). Glasgow, 1975–6.

Coles, K. Adlard. *Channel Harbours and Anchorages*. 5th ed. Nautical Publishing, 1977.

——. *Creeks and Harbours of the Solent*. 8th ed. Nautical Publishing 1972.

——. *North Brittany Pilot*. 3rd ed. Adlard Coles, 1977.

——. *North Sea Harbours and Pilotage* (Calais to den Helder). Adlard Coles, 1977.

Coles, K. A. and Black, A. N. *North Biscay Pilot*. Adlard Coles, 1977.

Coote, Jack H. *East Coast Rivers*. 8th ed. Yachting Monthly, 1977.

Cruising Association. *Visiting Yachtsman's Guide to the London River*. revised ed., 1977.

Denham, H. M. *The Aegean*. 3rd ed. John Murray, 1975.

——. *The Ionian Islands*. John Murray, 1972. (2nd ed. to be published summer 1978.)

Esmonde-Evans, David. *Cruising Association Handbook*. Cruising Association, 1971.

Irish Cruising Club. *Sailing Directions: East and North Coasts of Ireland*. 5th ed. 1970.

——. *Sailing Directions: South and West Coasts of Ireland.*

Kemp, Robert. *Irish Sea Cruising Guide*. Adlard Coles, 1976.

Kline, Harry, ed. *Yachtsman's Guide to the Bahamas*. Coral Gables, Florida: Tropic Isles Publishers, 1975.

Reed's Nautical Almanac 1978: American East-Coast Edition (Halifax, Nova Scotia, to Mexican Border, including the Islands). Thomas Reed Publications, 1977.

Royal Northumberland Yacht Club. *Sailing Directions: Humber Estuary to Rattray Head.*

Shaw, Capt. T. W. B., ed. *Sail West.* Devon: West of England Press, 1973.

Townsend, Stan. *Baltic Pilot.* Adlard Coles, 1972.

Wilson, W. T. *The Yachtsman's Pilot: Antwerp to Boulogne.* Imray, 1973.

NOTE: Local charts and sailing directions are obtainable from a number of clubs, which should be contracted direct.

CAVEAT: *This list was as up-to-date as possible at the time of going to press, but two things must be stressed. Whenever you buy a chart or other nautical document or book, make sure it is the latest edition and that you receive any supplements, etc., available. Because of the need for updating, most of the publications listed may be temporarily unavailable or out of print at any given moment. You will often be able to obtain a copy of the last edition at a second-hand bookshop, and it is well worth the effort.*